Employment and Lab
South Asia

Employment and Labour in South Asia

T. Anant
K. Sundaram
S. Tendulkar

South Asia Multidisciplinary Advisory Team (SAAT)
International Labour Organisation (ILO)
New Delhi - 110 003, India

Preface

Judged by the standards of the developing countries, the South Asian countries achieved fairly decent rates of economic growth over the past two decades. Yet the "employment problem" remains serious in all of them. The challenges confronting these countries at the present juncture, moreover, are formidable. Labour force growth is accelerating and will remain high in most countries of the region for quite sometime. If the "employment problem" is not to worsen, therefore, either economic growth must accelerate or growth must become more employment-intensive than it had been in the past, or both must occur.

These observations define the context for this study. It analyses the past experience with a view to identifying policy ideas for the future. The study begins by examining the past patterns of growth in employment and their relationship to the process of economic growth. The main conclusions emerging from this analysis can be briefly stated as follows. In all the countries, the high-productivity modern or organised sector failed to generate employment at a rate higher than that of the labour force growth. As a result, the burden of absorbing much of the incremental labour force fell on the low-productivity sectors such as agriculture and informal non-agricultural sectors, which already had substantial surplus labour and poor working conditions. The overall employment conditions could hardly be expected to improve in these circumstances. This also means that the problems of child labour and gender inequalities could not be effectively overcome.

The question naturally arises as to why the modern sectors failed to generate employment at an adequate pace. The authors suggest two main reasons - rigidities in the organised labour market and inward orientation of industrialisation strategies.

The domain of influence of labour policies in these countries is the organised sector, which typically accounts for less than ten per cent of the total employment. The study argues that this domain, rigid legal frameworks of employment protection and wage settlements, inadequate mechanisms of dispute settlement and weak systems of collective bargaining, combined to make employment and wage adjustments in response to changes in market conditions, extremely difficult. There were, thus, strong incentives for adoption of capital- and technology-intensive methods of production. These acted as constraints on employment growth in the organised sector.

Inward orientation of industrialisation strategies was also responsible for the low employment intensity of growth in the organised sectors in all countries other than perhaps Sri Lanka. Import substitution strategies generally placed emphasis on heavy industries, which tended to be capital-intensive in character. Such strategies also resulted in relatively slow overall economic growth, as this had to be supported by home market alone. Overall, import-substitutive strategies produced both slow growth and low employment intensity in the organised sector.

Rapid economic growth with effective and efficient labour utilisation can take these countries a long way in achieving the target of development and employment growth. This would define a macro-economic environment for the economies to participate in an international division of labour and also bring changes in labour institutions so as to permit flexibility in the labour market. Such a policy would permit efficient allocation and use of different inputs and reduce unit costs. The authors also point towards the need to establish adequate mechanisms of cost-sharing and conflict resolution to minimise the adverse impact on those who may be retrenched or otherwise affected by labour reforms.

These analytical findings have strong implications for future policies, and it is hoped that the monograph would contribute to the on-going debate on economic reforms and labour in South Asia

A. S. OBERAI
Director
July 1999 South Asia Multidisciplinary Advisory Team (SAAT)
New Delhi International Labour Organisation (ILO)

Contents

1 Introduction

The provision of gainful employment to a large and rapidly growing labour force at levels of productivity that are adequate to ensure acceptable levels of living represents a major challenge to policy makers throughout South Asia. A response to this challenge calls for an appreciation of both the key problems and constraints of the past several years as well as the current policy context of globalization and liberalization. The opportunities that present themselves to policy makers flow from the prospect of rapid expansion of international trade, and of outputs and value added in line with comparative advantage and the possibility of expansion in the volume of employment flowing therefrom. The challenge lies in limiting the damage to existing employment in the face of greater competition, and protecting, if not enhancing, the gains realized so far in the quality of employment: in terms of wages, security of tenure and other conditions of employment. Here again, there is scope for policy makers in South Asia to learn about the trade-offs inherent in these choices.

The present study analyzes these issues in four chapters. Chapter 2 reviews the broad trends in employment and unemployment in South Asia[1] against the backdrop of the past trends and outlook for expansion in the size of the workforce. This is preceded by a brief but critical review of concepts used and practices followed in resolving issues of measurement to impart the necessary balance and caution necessary for cross-country comparisons.

Chapter 3 primarily deals with labour market institutions in some of the countries of South Asia. It covers the institutional setting governing both employment conditions and wage determination and examines the issue of labour market flexibility which has acquired importance in the current context of globalization and liberalization.

---

1. Throughout the study, South Asia refers to the five countries under discussion: Bangladesh, India, Nepal, Pakistan and Sri Lanka.

The chapter highlights the different dimensions of the concept of flexibility and how rigidities in some dimensions are often accompanied by and at times lead to flexibility in other areas.

Chapter 4 assesses the employment effects of trade liberalization adopted in different degrees by the countries of the region. In addition to the discussion at the aggregate level, the chapter includes case studies of two sectors in India which have been associated with rapid growth, namely, readymade garments and leather.

Finally, Chapter 5 draws on the analysis of the preceding sections to highlight some of the key problems and policy options before governments in the region in meeting the challenge of converting the rapidly rising labour force into a productive force for rapid economic development and the alleviation and eventual elimination of poverty.

2 Size and Structure of Employment and Unemployment in South Asia

This chapter brings together and analyzes the available evidence on different facets of employment and unemployment in five countries of South Asia - Bangladesh, India, Nepal, Pakistan and Sri Lanka - since the early 1980s (Table 2.1).

Productivity of the workforce is a key concern when analyzing the structure and dynamics of the employed population. Low productivity follows from the simple identity that per capita income is the product of per worker productivity and the worker population ratio (WPR). WPR being a ratio, varies within narrow bounds for the same country over time, or in inter-country comparisons. Low living standards indicated by low per capita income are thus directly attributed to low worker productivity. From this perspective, it is important to examine the distribution of the workforce across, at least, broad industry divisions seen against the distribution of Gross Domestic Product across the same industry divisions.

For meaningful inter-sectoral and inter-country comparisons of productivity levels, we combine this analysis with estimates of average productivity of the workforce in the economy as a whole at comparable purchasing power parity (PPP) dollars for a recent year, 1994. Further, in order to help identify commonalities across South Asia and to target policy intervention, we also explore the divide between self-employed and wage-employed, and, within the latter, between casual labour and regular salaried/ wage employees categorized by gender, age and, to the extent feasible, formal and informal segments. The analysis of the size and structure of the workforce is complemented by an examination of the nature and extent of unemployment in the countries under discussion.

Our review of the available evidence in South Asia throws up some positive developments:

◆ a decline in the share of the low-productivity agriculture sector in the workforce;

◆ rising real product per worker in all sectors of the economy; and,
◆ generally rising levels of real wage rates.

The key areas of concern for policy planners in South Asia include:
◆ high levels of illiteracy and, even among the literates, low levels of educational attainment of the workforce in the Indian subcontinent;
◆ high levels of open unemployment in Sri Lanka; and,
◆ a pattern of labour absorption where high-productivity sectors fail to absorb an adequate share of the expanding labour force while sectors with low levels of product per worker absorb labour at a rate faster than the growth in their value added.

2.1 Some Key Issues in Measurement

Population Censuses and Labour Force Surveys form the basic database for analyses of employment and unemployment in South Asia. However, over time, labour force (sample) surveys have emerged as the principal data sources.

In assessing the coverage and comparability of estimates emerging from different labour force surveys both across countries and within countries over time, a number of key issues relating to concepts and measurement need to be addressed. Two questions, in particular, stand out: First, how adequately is participation in economic activity captured in data? Second, how reliable are available estimates of unemployment in reflecting the true extent of involuntary non-participation in economic activity?

2.1.1 Concept of Employment

A clear understanding of the concept of productive or gainful employment or participation in economic activity and its counterpart, unemployment, is essential. In all the countries of South Asia, a substantial proportion of the value added is generated in household enterprises where the bulk of the labour input is provided by own-account workers and family workers who do not receive any wages as a *quid pro quo* for the services provided. To account for this factor, the concept of gainful work or employment must go beyond activities that involve receipt of income for work and cover a notion that encompasses "work for family gain". This extended concept has been adopted in the labour force surveys of all the countries of the region.

To take cognizance of the presence, in varying degrees, of production entirely for self-consumption or subsistence production in almost all countries of South Asia (with the possible exception of Sri Lanka), a further extension of the concept of employment is necessary. However, an unqualified extension of the concept of employment to cover all activities that result in increased consumption by the family of goods and services would render it non-operational. Virtually no activity would remain outside the boundary of employment if so defined and the entire population, other than the too young and the too old would need to be considered as being at work or employed. A convenient practice to resolve this problem has been to rely on the accounting conventions used in the United Nations System of National Accounts (SNA).

Since 1968 and prior to the 1993 SNA, all production in the primary sector, processing of home-grown primary products entirely for self-consumption, and, own-account production of fixed assets were treated as falling within the sphere of economic activity. The labour input for such production activity was treated as productive work. In the 1993 SNA, the coverage of subsistence production was extended to cover *all* goods and only the simultaneous production and immediate self-consumption of *services* were treated as falling outside the boundary of economic activity.

Jacob (1986) and Sundaram (1989) have evaluated the methods of data collection adopted in the Population Censuses and Labour Force Surveys of India with reference to coverage and ability to implement under field conditions, the concept of economic activity, as also the concept of employment as it exists in tune with the (pre-1993) System of National Accounts. These evaluation exercises have revealed that the labour force surveys better cover productive employment and economic activity and are also in line with the UNSNA as compared to the population censuses. They point out that population censuses are carried out by ad hoc investigators (with very little training) whose workload does not permit them to spend time with every household covered by the census. Labour force sample surveys (LFSS) on the other hand, are usually carried out by experienced and trained full-time investigators who spend longer periods with each (selected sample) household to probe and ascertain participation in economic activity. This is particularly important from the perspective of capturing the participation of women and children in economic activity.

Such explicit comparisons do not exist for population censuses and labour force surveys carried out in the other countries of South Asia. However, the impact of adopting broader concepts and definitions has resulted in better estimates of women's participation in economic activity in both Bangladesh and Pakistan. The impact has been particularly dramatic in the case of Bangladesh. The use of a broader definition of work in the 1989 Labour Force Survey was shown to raise the labour force participation rate

(LFPR) among women aged 10 years and above from 10.6 per cent to 63.4 per cent. This raises the question whether the results of the 1989 and subsequent labour force surveys are at all comparable with those for earlier years. An outright rejection of the results of earlier surveys deprives us of a reference point for the early 1980s. Using them with caution may be preferable to completely jettisoning them. Though less dramatic, changes in concepts and definitions adopted in the 1990-91 labour force survey of Pakistan have resulted in raising the estimates of female LFPR for that country.

The inclusion of activities captured by broadening the concept of employment that primarily relate to production for family gain and subsistence production, chiefly in agriculture and allied activities, affect not only LFPR, especially of women and children, but also change the structure of employment in general and the industrial distribution of the workforce in particular. Here again, Bangladesh provides the most dramatic example: between the 1984-85 and the 1989 labour force surveys, the share of agriculture and allied activities by the female workforce jumped from 9.3 per cent to 71.5 per cent, while the share of the "household sector" fell from 43.7 per cent in 1984-85 to 3.3 per cent in 1989. Clearly, caution needs to be exercised in comparisons of the size and structure of the workforce of Bangladesh between 1984-85 and 1989.

2.1.2 Concept of Unemployment

Having examined the concept of 'gainful unemployment', we now turn to its counterpart, namely, unemployment. Central to the concept of unemployment is the notion of involuntary non-participation in work. An obvious feature of 'involuntariness' is that the person makes an effort to find work or should be seeking work. However, in a situation where there are no perceived opportunities for gainful employment, a person may not actively seek work and yet report his/her availability for work if work were available. This concept has been recognized in estimating unemployment by all the countries of South Asia. The concept of unemployment used in labour force surveys has now been broadened to include all those not having gainful employment *and* either reported to be seeking work *or*, if not seeking work, reported to be available for work. In Pakistan, until 1990-91, labour force surveys recorded persons as unemployed who were without work (i.e., not in paid employment or self-employment) and *both* currently available *and seeking* work during the reference period of one week. In particular, those available but not seeking work were not recorded as unemployed.

Since 1990-91, the condition of being available for work (whether or not actively seeking work) is sufficient for a person to be recorded as unemployed. This resulted in the unemployment rate (unemployed as a proportion of persons in the labour force) jumping from 3.1 per cent in 1989-90 to 6.3 per cent in 1990-91. This means that, for Pakistan, unemployment rates before 1990-91 and after 1990-91 are strictly not comparable.

2.1.3 Measurement of Employment and Unemployment

Moving away from concepts, let us consider a few key issues that arise in the measurement of employment and unemployment. First, there is the question of the cut-off age applied to the population covered in labour force surveys. Except in India, where only the population in age group 0-4 is excluded, in all the other countries of South Asia the population coverage in the labour force surveys is restricted to those aged 10 years or more. This would restrict the estimates of child labour to the population in the age group 10-14 years in all the countries of the region, except in India where child workers in the age group 5-9 years are also covered in the surveys. In practical terms, however, this does not introduce a major source of discrepancy in the estimates of child labour across the countries of South Asia. By 1993-94 the LFPR among children in the 5-9 age group was only 5 per 1,000 in urban areas in India for both boys and girls, and 11 and 14 per 1,000, respectively, for boys and girls in rural India. At the same time, numerically, as many as 1.2 million of the 13.1 million children in the labour force in India in 1993-94 were in the age group of 5-9 years.

Another key issue in the measurement of employment and unemployment is the length of the reference period. Typically, labour force surveys have a short reference period not exceeding 15 days preceding the date of the interview. The resulting estimates are referred to as the 'current status' estimates. In all the countries of South Asia, current status estimates have a reference period of seven days preceding the date of interview. Two of the countries, India and Sri Lanka, also collect information on 'usual status' with a reference period of 365 days preceding the date of interview. This is in recognition of the fact that in these economies the current status of an individual may differ significantly from his/her usual status. In addition, in India, the quinquennial labour force surveys also collect information on the activity status of individuals for *each* of the seven days of the reference week, and the resultant estimates are referred to as 'daily status' estimates.

A comparison of LFPRs across alternative reference periods in India and Sri Lanka (Table 2.2) reveals differences in the pattern of variations. In India, the workforce participation rates fall and the unemployment rates (as a proportion of labour force) rise as we move from usual to current weekly and current daily status. In Sri Lanka, such a transition from usual to current (weekly) status shows a rise in WFPR and a fall in the unemployment rate. Parallel contrasts are also seen in respect of LFPRs. It is, however, noteworthy that in India the differences in LFPR as we move from usual to current status are lower in 1993-94 compared to 1983. In Sri Lanka, too, the differences narrowed over the period 1990 to 1996.

Given that LFPRs are higher under usual status in India than under current status, while the converse is true for Sri Lanka, the choice of usual status estimates for detailed tabulation of labour force characteristics in India and current status estimates in Sri Lanka seem to be appropriate. The usual status estimates, however, raise two kinds of problems. First, with the long reference period of 365 days preceding the date of interview, a given individual may be economically active (or be at work) for part of the year, be unemployed for another part of the year and, in principle, be out of the labour force for the remaining part of the year. In India, beginning with the 32nd Round of the National Sample Survey (NSS)(1977-78), this problem was resolved by the adoption of the majority time criterion to define what is referred to as 'usual principal status'. However, in order to capture the labour force contribution of those not in the workforce on principal status in India, a further classification of such persons has been devised depending on whether or not they were in the labour force as per 'subsidiary status' as defined by their attachment to the labour force more or less regularly for some time in the year. A detailed tabulation of labour force characteristics is provided for this inclusive (principal plus subsidiary status) category in NSS.

The second problem regarding usual status estimates arises from the fact that, apart from those not at work on the majority time criterion, some proportion of those at work by principal status also engage in other economic activities by subsidiary status.[1] Estimates now available for the NSS 50th Round (1993-94) for India show that, among both males and females in rural areas, a little over one-third of those who are employed as per principal status are engaged in some subsidiary economic activity as well. In urban

---

1. Over a larger reference period of 365 days, it is possible that a person may be engaged in more than one subsidiary activity besides the major time spent in the reported principal status. In the forthcoming quinquennial NSS of Employment and Unemployment it is proposed to record two subsidiary activities from persons apart from their principal activity.

areas, this proportion is about 6 per cent in the aggregate but close to 21 per cent for those employed in agricultural activities. These tabulations also show that workers engaged in subsidiary economic activity are mostly self-employed, with casual labour as the second largest segment. With reference to industry of attachment, subsidiary activity is predominantly in agriculture for rural males and females and urban females, while it is equally divided between agriculture and non-agriculture for urban males.

Another perspective on the issue of industry of attachment is provided by a comparison of the share of agriculture and allied activities in the workforce under alternative reference periods. This is possible only for India, as the available results from the Sri Lankan labour force survey do not provide the industrial distribution of the usual status workforce. Results from India show that, along with a decline in the overall workforce participation rates as we move from usual to current weekly and from current weekly to current daily status, there is a decline in the share of agriculture and allied activities in the workforce. This is true both for the early 1980s and 1990s. Thus, in 1993-94, the share of agriculture in the workforce declined from about 64 per cent under usual status (PS+SS) to 61 per cent under current weekly status and to 60 per cent under current daily status. These estimates also suggest that, at least in terms of a broad agriculture-non-agriculture division of the workforce, the industry of attachment of the workers remains fairly stable within the reference week.

In labour force surveys that have a week as the reference period, it is a common practice to use the priority rule for resolving the problem of multiplicity of activity status of an individual. Under this, the status of being at work has priority over that of being unemployed, with the latter, in turn, having priority over the status of being outside the labour force. The practice of collecting information in units of half-a-day while recording information on the activity status of an individual for each of the seven days of the reference week followed in India should mitigate if not eliminate the problem of multiplicity of status within a day.

The use of the priority rule opens up the question of underemployment during the reference week for those classified as currently employed. In Bangladesh, Nepal, Pakistan and Sri Lanka this is sought to be captured by a classification of those in the workforce by hours worked during the reference week. Since those with a job or an enterprise but not at work during the week are also classified as part of the workforce, they are recorded as having worked 'zero' hours while determining their current status. Excluding this category, and applying some (inherently arbitrary) cut-off in terms of number of hours worked per week, the underemployed among the employed are identified. In Bangladesh, Nepal and Sri Lanka the cut-off level is 40 hours per week, while in Pakistan it is specified as 35 hours per week. In India, no information is collected (since 1972-73) on hours worked. Instead, as previously indicated, information about activity status is collected for each of the seven days of the week with a half-day as the primary time unit. In this case, a 35-hours cut-off can be approximated by those working for a four and half days or less per week and a 40-hour cut-off by those working for five days or less during the reference week.

The simultaneous canvassing of information on the activity status of an individual over alternative reference periods, as in India and Sri Lanka, opens up the possibility of alternative indicators of underemployment through cross-tabulation. Thus, tabulation of the labour force survey data in India makes possible the estimation of the proportion of those in the workforce as per usual status (either principal or subsidiary status) who are classified as unemployed (seeking or available for work) by weekly status (using the priority criterion) or daily status. Similarly, it is possible to measure the extent of open unemployment (on daily status) among those classified as being in the workforce on weekly status. This is sometimes referred to as visible underemployment among the employed (on usual or weekly status). This measure has the advantage of reflecting the status of seeking and/or available for work as reported by the respondent which is not the case when we use an inherently arbitrary cut-off level of hours worked.

The fact that some proportion of those in the workforce during the reference week (as per the priority rule) do not report to be seeking and/or are available for work on days (during the reference week) when they are not at work and hence can be classified as being outside the labour force, has raised the question whether they are to be viewed as discouraged dropouts. Discouraged dropouts are those who are so discouraged by the non-availability of work as to not even report to be seeking or available for work. However, as Visaria (1990) has argued, "Such a presumption is unwarranted because real life includes many compulsions when a person is forced to drop out of the labour force for a part of the reference week", especially in the case of "persons who do not enjoy 'casual leave' or paid absence from work".

In India, a set of probing questions is asked of those classified as outside the labour force on the basis of usual status by the majority time criterion. The questions were addressed to students, those engaged in household duties and others outside the labour force (OLF) on the basis of usual (principal) status. They were asked whether they were available for work, and if so, the nature of efforts made by them to find such work.

Those (among the OLF as per usual principal status (PS) who declared themselves to be seeking or available for work would be classified as unemployed by usual subsidiary status (SS) or as unemployed during the reference week and therefore as unemployed by daily status. They would thus be classified as part of the labour force on extended (PS+SS) usual status. And, if reported to be seeking or available for work on even one half-day during the reference week, they would belong to the labour force on the basis of current weekly and current daily status by the priority criterion.

In respect of those (among the OLF by the usual principal status) who reported seeking or available for work in response to the probing questions, any one classified as being engaged in household duties, in usual principal status, likely to contribute to family income, though not so for the major part of the year, could be captured as part of the labour force on extended usual (PS+SS) status.

Women engaged in household duties (according to usual principal status) were also asked about their availability for work "inside" (rather than outside) the home, the type and nature of such work and possible assistance required for the purpose. In so far as respondents interpret "seeking or available for work" as relating to *paid work* outside the household, this probing question could help identify availability for participation in work not captured in the main survey. In 1993-94, of the women (aged 15 years or more) usually engaged (i.e. on the majority time criterion) in the household duties (56 per cent in rural India and 65 per cent in urban India), 30 per cent in rural India and 27 per cent in urban India reported availability for work in the premises of their home. Of these, again, 68 per cent in rural India and 63 per cent in urban India preferred only "part time work" on a regular basis, while 27 and 33 per cent respectively in rural and urban India preferred full time work.

Indian surveys also make possible two other indicators of underemployment through what are called "probing questions". One question addressed to those in the workforce on usual (principal) status attempts to ascertain whether the respondent is "more or less fully engaged in work during the last 365 days". Those answering 'yes' would presumably not be underemployed whereas those answering 'no' would be. Those answering 'no' are further classified by reference to whether they sought or were available for work on most days, on some days or not at all. Clearly, the last category may be eliminated from the category of the underemployed by this criterion.

The 50th Round NSS (1993-94) in India, tabulates the "number of usually working (principal status) persons (15 years and above) who sought or were available for alternative work per 1,000 usually working (principal status) persons and their per 1,000 distribution by reason for seeking or availability for alternate work". This tabulation is provided separately by gender and by rural-urban location. And, one of the listed 'reasons' is "present work not remunerative enough". If we shift the focus of underemployment from unutilized labour time to perceived inadequacy of remuneration or returns to labour time spent, at least this sub-category of those seeking or available for alternative work may also be categorized as underemployed. On the basis of this criterion, between 2 to 3 per cent of the usual status adult workforce in India has been found to be underemployed.

2.2 Participation Rates and Size of Workforce

Bangladesh, India, Nepal, Pakistan and Sri Lanka, taken together, had an estimated civilian workforce of a little under half a billion (484.5 million) in the early 1990s. With over 374 million workers, India accounts for an overwhelming share of South Asia's workers, while Sri Lanka has the smallest size of workforce - a little over 5 million (Table 2.1).

Underlying the estimates of the workforce are (crude) worker-population ratios (WPRs) that vary significantly across countries and by gender. For females, the WPRs (per 1,000) range from 66 in Pakistan to 448 in Nepal. In the case of males, the range is from 544 in India to 442 in Pakistan (Table 2.2).

A comparison of WPRs over time (excluding Bangladesh for reasons of non-comparability) shows that, between the early 1980s and the early 1990s, WPRs have changed only marginally in India (a decline from 421 to 418 per 1,000) and in Sri Lanka (an increase from 317 to 322 per 1,000). More substantial changes are seen in Nepal and Pakistan. In Nepal, the crude WPR rose from 456 to 471 per 1,000 between 1981 and 1991 (as per the ILO estimates for 1991). In Pakistan, by contrast, WPRs fell from 302 per 1,000 in 1982-83 to 260 per 1,000 in 1994-95 (Table 2.3).

The rise in the crude WPRs in Nepal occurred despite a significant fall in WPRs for males (from 583 to 493 per 1,000) which is more than offset by the rise in WPRs for females from 323 to 448 per 1,000. This rise in female WPRs appears to be largely a consequence of the ability of the 'living standard measurement survey' (LSMS) 1995-96 by the ILO to better capture women's participation in the workforce. Thus, the 1995-96 LSMS reports close to 66 per cent of rural females (aged 10 and over) to be in the workforce compared to 47 per cent estimated by the 1981 and 1991 population censuses. For urban females, the differences are less sharp between the 1981 population census and the 1995-96 LSMS. The decline in crude WPRs for males reflects the fairly sharp decline in WPRs in the 10-14 and 15-19 age groups (presumably reflecting greater participation in schooling), as also a reduction in WPR in the 60+ age group.

In the case of Pakistan, part of the explanation for the decline in the crude WPRs lies in the reduction in the share of those aged 10 and over in the total population. This decline, from 687 to 664 per 1,000, has taken place despite a marginal increase in the share of the urban 10+ population from 198 to 202 per 1,000. The fall in the share of the rural population aged 10 and above in the total (all areas) population from 488 to 461 per 1,000 may be a consequence of age-selective out-migration of adults from rural Pakistan against the backdrop of a more or less constant rate of growth of population. Another contributing factor, *albeit* minor, would be the small rise in the share of the urban population (from 283 to 288 per 1,000).

Apart from these changes in the age distribution and in the rural-urban composition of the population, the principal factor underlying the decline in the crude WPRs in Pakistan is a significant reduction in the age-specific worker-population rates in the 10-14 (from 215 to 115 per 1,000); 15-19 (403 to 323 per 1,000); and the 20-24 (from 508 to 479 per 1,000) age groups. It may be expected that these declines in WPRs are matched by increased participation in schooling/higher education.

Underlying the marginal changes in worker-population ratios in Sri Lanka are significant changes in the age structure of the population as well as changes in age-sex-specific participation rates. Not only has the share of children (0-14 age-group) fallen from 352 to 280 per 1,000 between 1981 (census) and 1996 (projection) but also that of young adults (15-25 years) has fallen from 211 to 187 per 1,000. At the other end, the share of the population in the 35-59 age group has risen from 209 to 281 per 1,000, while that of the 60+ age group has risen from 66 to 90 per 1,000. Except for the rise in the share of the 60+ age-group, the other changes in the age structure of the Sri Lankan population tend to push up the participation rates overall.

In the case of Sri Lanka, it is also noteworthy that the age-specific (labour force) participation rates of females in the 15-19 and 20-24 age groups have gone up between 1981 and 1996. The rise is particularly sharp in the 20-24 age group (from 359 to 432 per 1,000). In the case of males, however, the LFPR in the 15-19 age group fell from 415 to 338 per 1,000, while it rose from 800 to 833 per 1,000 in the 20-24 age group. Overall, while male WPRs have fallen, those of women have risen.

In the Indian case too, the shift in the age-structure of the population towards the prime working ages has tended to soften the impact of falling LFPRs in the 10-14, 15-19 and 20-24 age groups.

2.3 Outlook for the Future

The labour force growth that is expected to occur over the next 15 to 20 years will be shaped by: (a) the pace of population growth, which is expected to be slower than in the past; (b) the consequent shift in age structure of the population towards the prime working age groups; (c) the possibility of a decline in (age-specific) participation rates among the younger age groups due to increased participation in schooling; and, (d) the expected rise in LFPRs of women in the working age groups in the context of the projected decline in the fertility burden and general development.

The projections are summarized in the table below:

Projected Growth of Labour Force in South Asia

Country	Period	Rate of Growth of LF per annum)	Annual Addition to LF (million)
Bangladesh	1990-2010	1.71	1.0
India	1997-2012	2.26	10.6
Nepal	1996-2011	2.70	0.3
Pakistan	1997-2012	2.75	1.25
Sri Lanka	1996-2011	1.25	0.08

Among the countries of South Asia, Sri Lanka is most favourably placed as far as the expected labour force expansion over the next 15-20 years is concerned. With a low rate of growth of population of 1 per cent per annum, the slowing down in that rate of growth and the consequential shift in the age structure towards the prime age groups may be expected to be moderate. While there is some scope for a rise in labour force participation rates among women in the prime age groups, the scope for a reduction in participation rates among the younger age groups due to rising school enrolment would be limited. On balance, the prospects are for a labour force expansion of between 1 and 1.25 per cent per annum. From a level of about 6.25 million (excluding the Northern and the Eastern Provinces) in 1996, the labour force in Sri Lanka may be projected to be about 7.5 million by 2011.

This would imply an average annual increment of only about 0.08 million.

In terms of current rates of population growth, Nepal and Pakistan are at the other end of the spectrum among the countries of South Asia. ILO-SAAT[2] has assumed a population growth rate of close to 2.7 per cent per annum in the population and labour force for 1996. Projecting the labour force to grow at the same rate till 2011 would raise Nepal's labour force from about 10.5 million in 1996 to 15.6 million in 2011. This would imply an increment in the labour force by a little over 0.3 million per annum.

In Pakistan too, labour force estimates for 1996 imply an annual compound rate of growth of about 2.6 per cent between 1991 and 1996, while those for 1997 as reported by ILO-SAAT[3] imply a growth of about 2.8 per cent per annum over the estimate for 1996. Projected at a growth rate of 2.75 per cent per annum, Pakistan's labour force would reach a level of 55.8 million in 2012, compared to about 37.2 million in 1997. This would imply that over this period, on an average, close to 1.25 million would be added every year to Pakistan's labour force.

The World Bank's population projections for Bangladesh suggest a significant slowdown in the rate of population growth in Bangladesh from a level close to 2 per cent per annum during the 1990-95 quinquennium to about 1.4 per cent per annum during the 2005-2010 quinquennium. This would imply an annual average rate of growth of about 1.6 per cent per annum between 1955 and 2010 and of about 1.7 per cent per annum between 1990-2010. Assuming that the age structure will shift towards the prime age groups and the lower participation rates among the younger age groups due to greater schooling will roughly offset each other, and with the female participation rates already at a high level and not expected to rise further, a rate of growth of the labour force of about 1.71 per cent per annum is possible. This would imply that, starting with an estimated labour force of about 51.20 million in 1990, Bangladesh would have about 71.7 million people in the civilian labour force by 2010. On the basis of these projections, a little over 1 million would be added every year to the labour force in Bangladesh.

In a recent study, Pravin Visaria (1997) has made labour force projections for India for the period 1997 to 2012. According to this study, India's labour force, estimated at 399 million in 1997, is projected to rise to a level of about 558 million by 2012. Over the three quinquennia, the net additions to labour force, which will peak at a little over 11 million per annum, will average at 10.6 million per annum. Net additions in the 2007-12 quinquennium will

---

2. ILO-SAAT (1997a).
3. ILO-SAAT (1997b).

comprise fresh entrants to the tune of 16.4 million, offset by exits from the labour force at the rate of about 5.9 million per annum. These projections also indicate that during the period 2007-12, a little over 5 million of the new entrants each year would be women. If women's participation rates rise over time, these figures could be even larger.

2.4 Industrial Distribution and Productivity of theWorkforce

Almost all the countries of the region experienced a significant decline in the share of agriculture and allied activities between the early 1980s and 1990s (Table 2.4). The only apparent exception is Bangladesh. The decline in the share of agriculture was compensated largely by an increase in the share of services, with the manufacturing sector gaining little: in Pakistan, the share of the mining and manufacturing sector, in fact, shows a 2.5 per cent decline between 1982-83 and 1993-94. Gains by the infrastructure sectors, if any, have been marginal.

Before considering the question of comparative levels of productivity of the workforce in the major industrial groups across three countries (Table 2.5), it is important to note that the measure used is fairly simple, even crude, that is, average value added per worker at comparable purchasing power parity (PPP) dollars.

Our approach to deriving a set of comparable estimates of labour productivity takes as its starting point the estimates of per capita GDP at comparable PPP dollars for 1994.[4]

In the next step, estimates of GDP per capita at PPP dollars are converted into *per worker* values for the economy as a whole using the crude worker-population ratios for 1994. Here, the problem of using WPRs of different countries poses a problem. Crude WPRs include female WPRs that are as low as 66 per 1,000 in Pakistan and as high as 448 in Nepal (Table 2.3). In Sri Lanka female WPRs are 195 per 1,000 while they are 283 per 1,000 in India. These differences are, in our judgement, largely reflective of the differences in concepts and definitions used in the different labour force surveys. To ensure greater comparability across countries, the conversion of GDP per capita into GDP per worker (for all industries taken together), is carried out by using the worker-population ratios for *males*. Further, to ensure comparability across countries of South Asia, the WPRs used for India have been measured by current weekly status, as in the case of Pakistan and Sri Lanka, even though for India, estimates of WPR by usual status are also available.

---

4. These are available in UNDP(1994).

Secondly, the *relative* labour productivity in a given industry group (relative to the average GDP per worker for the economy as a whole) is obtained as the *ratio* of share of the industry group(s) in GDP (in local currency units) to its share in the workforce of both sexes taken together. A degree of non-comparability across countries arises from the fact that, for India, the detailed industrial distribution is available only in respect of the workforce defined by reference to usual status (with a reference period of 365 days preceding the date of interview) and *not* for that defined by weekly status. As we had seen earlier (Table 2.1), the share of agriculture and allied activities in the workforce by weekly status is lower (at 612 for 1,000) than its share in the workforce by usual status (639 per 1,000). This would imply that, for India, comparable *relative* labour productivity (relative to the national average) would be higher than indicated for agriculture and allied activities and lower than indicated for the non-agricultural sector.

As a final comment on the methodology used, it may be noted that, in all cases, no adjustment has been made for the differential degree of weekly underemployment across industry groups. This is dictated by the absence of relevant data for India.

The estimates of sectoral labour productivity, in terms of comparable PPP dollars, for 1994, are presented in Table 2.3. It is seen that productivity levels of the Sri Lankan workforce are higher than those for India and Pakistan, and those for Pakistan are higher than for India. This is true for all the broad industry groups. This in turn follows from the higher value of GDP per capita (in PPP dollars) in Sri Lanka relative to India and Pakistan, and in Pakistan relative to India. These differences are magnified (in terms of GDP per worker) by the lower WPR for males in Sri Lanka relative to India and Pakistan relative to India.

In order to track the changes over time in the relative (to economy-wide average) and absolute levels of labour productivity (as measured by value added per worker) and in the extent of inter-sectoral inequality in labour productivity, we present a more detailed industrial distribution of the workforce and of GDP, along with estimates of GDP (in domestic currency units) and workforce for two (Sri Lanka) or three (India and Pakistan) time points (see Tables 2.6, 2.7, and 2.8).

Before examining the changes over time in relative labour productivity in major industry divisions at one-digit detail in the three countries, a brief comment on the index of relative labour productivity in the agriculture and construction sectors in India, as compared to Pakistan and Sri Lanka would be in order.

As noted earlier, in India, the detailed industrial distribution relates to estimates of the workforce on the basis of usual status with a reference period of 365 days preceding the date of interview; and that the share of agriculture and allied activities is higher for the usual status workforce as compared to its share in the workforce estimated as per current weekly or current daily status. In comparison with both Pakistan and Sri Lanka, where the industrial distribution relates to the employed population by current (weekly) status, the share of the agriculture and allied activities sector in the workforce would be artificially higher, and therefore the index of relative labour productivity lower in India as compared to Pakistan and Sri Lanka.

In view of the above, the slightly higher value of the index of relative labour productivity of the agricultural sector in Pakistan relative to India in the early 1980s and in Sri Lanka relative to India in the early 1990s, would be more apparent than real. This is, however, not true of the differences in the index of relative labour productivity of the agricultural sector in the 1990s as between India (0.49) and Pakistan (0.56).

Given the fact that, in the slack agricultural season, many of those classified as belonging to the agricultural sector by usual status in fact seek and find work in the non-agricultural sector in general and in construction activities in particular, the index of relative labour productivity of the non-agricultural sector in general and in construction in particular would tend to be (artificially) higher in India than in Pakistan and Sri Lanka. Notwithstanding this, it is noteworthy that the index of relative labour productivity in the construction sector is sharply higher in India than in Pakistan. Significantly, for a comparable period, this index is higher for Sri Lanka than for both India and Pakistan. Apart from reflecting possible differences in the technologies used and, perhaps the rural-urban composition of construction activity, these inter-country differences in the index of relative labour productivity are also indicative of the extent to which this sector is serving as a residual absorber of the expanding labour force in the three countries.

Turning to the changes in relative labour productivities in different sectors (relative to the average product per worker in the economy as a whole), a feature common to all the three countries is the decline over time in the *relative* labour productivity of the agricultural sector. Given the fact that in all the three countries, the agricultural sector records the lowest level of relative (and hence also absolute) labour productivity, the failure of the sector's share in workforce to decline sufficiently to offset the decline in its share in GDP, suggests that the agricultural sector continues to play the role of residual absorber of the expanding workforce. On the positive side, it may be noted that the share of this low productivity sector has declined and, thanks to the overall growth in productivity, in absolute terms, the per worker productivity (at constant prices) has increased over time, *albeit* very slowly.

Apart from the agricultural (and allied activities) sector, the construction sector in Pakistan and the "other services" sector in Sri Lanka have an index of relative labour productivity less than 1, indicating levels of labour productivity below the economy wide average. Further, the share of the workforce in the construction sector in Pakistan, and of the 'other services' sector in Sri Lanka, have increased over time. Also, the rise in the share of these sectors in the workforce has been greater than the rise in the sectors' share in GDP. This suggests that the construction sector in Pakistan and the "other services" sector in Sri Lanka may be serving as residual absorbers of the expanding labour force in these two countries.

From the perspective of labour absorption, one of the key areas of concern in the Indian case has been the failure of the high productivity organized manufacturing sector to absorb the rapidly expanding workforce. From a level of 2.3 per cent of the workforce in the early 1970s and 1980s, the share of the organized or what in India is called the registered manufacturing sector in the workforce has in fact *declined, albeit* marginally, to 2.1 per cent. Against the background of a rise in this sector's share in GDP (from 10.2 to 13.6 per cent between 1972-73 and 1993-94), the virtual stagnation of the share of the registered manufacturing sector in the workforce has resulted in a rise in the index of this sector's relative labour productivity (from 4.5 to 6.6). This means that the model of economic transformation of economies with abundance of labour visualized by Arthur Lewis, where excess labour from the low productivity agricultural sector, as well as the expanding workforce get progressively absorbed in the high productivity modern industrial sector, has yet to happen in India.

A related feature of labour in the manufacturing sector in India is also noteworthy. Throughout the period, the unorganized sector, while absorbing a significantly larger share of the workforce than the registered (factory) sector, has a lower share in GDP. Not only that, over time, the relative position of the unorganized segment has worsened in relation to both the economy-wide average productivity and the organized manufacturing sector. Whereas the index of relative productivity of the registered manufacturing sector has risen from 4.5 to 6.7, for the unregistered segment this index has registered a decline from 1.14 to 0.9 between 1972-73 and 1993-94. This suggests that some measure of residual absorption of the expanding workforce in India is taking place in the unorganized manufacturing sector as well.

We have already noted a similar process in the agricultural sector.

Using the relative mean deviation as a summary measure of inequality of inter-sectoral labour productivity, it is seen that in India over the period 1972-73 to 1993-94, this inequality has widened from a level that is already the highest among the three countries. This has happened despite the fact that, with the exception of the registered manufacturing sector, the index of relative labour productivity has fallen in all the other sectors.

In Pakistan, inter-sectoral inequality in productivity per worker fell between 1984-85 and 1990-91. However, since then it has increased (in 1994-95) to a level slightly higher than that in 1984-85.

Over a much shorter period (1990-96) inter-sectoral inequalities in labour productivity have declined in Sri Lanka from 0.55 to 0.52.

2.5   Quality of Labour and Employment

An important element in the quality of workforce that impacts upon levels of productivity in the economy is the structure of the workforce in terms of the level of educational attainment. Estimates available for India, Pakistan and Sri Lanka for 1994 (see Table 2.9) show that both male and female workers in Sri Lanka are much better placed than their counterparts in India and Pakistan. While close to or above 50 per cent of the workers in India and Pakistan are illiterate, this proportion is less than 7 per cent in Sri Lanka.

In terms of gender differentials, women workers in Sri Lanka are better educated than their male counterparts (despite having a larger proportion of illiterates) insofar as a significantly larger proportion of women workers are 'graduates and above'. Women workers are distinctly worse off in terms of educational attainment in both India and Pakistan, with close to 75 per cent in India and about 81 per cent in Pakistan being illiterate. Male workers in India are better placed with a lower proportion of illiterate workers and a larger proportion with a 'graduate and above' level of education. In the case of females, while Pakistan has a larger proportion of illiterate women workers, it has also a somewhat larger proportion (10.6 per cent as opposed to 6.4 per cent) of women workers with 'secondary school and above' level of education.

Turning from the quality of the workforce to the quality of employment, we first examine the issue of underemployment (in terms of non-utilization of labour time) among those classified as part of the workforce by reference to the status prevailing in the reference week with the priority rule used for the resolution of multiple status. Table 2.10 presents estimates, wherever possible for two or more time points from the early 1980s and the early 1990s, of the prevalence rates of underemployment. Here, the underemployed are defined as those working less than 40 hours a week (or in the case of India, five days a week) during the reference week in Bangladesh, India, Nepal and Sri Lanka. In the case of Pakistan, the cut-off level is 35 hours of work during the reference week. Wherever the details are available, it excludes those who had a job (or an enterprise if self-employed) but did not work at all during the reference week. Typically, the extent of underemployment is greater in rural areas than in urban areas, and, with the exception of Pakistan, higher in the early 1990s than in the early 1980s. The rate of underemployment in the 1990s is the highest in Nepal followed by Sri Lanka, Bangladesh, India and Pakistan, in that order. As is to be expected, workers in the agriculture sector report the highest rates of underemployment. In Sri Lanka, mining and quarrying and construction also report relatively high rates of underemployment.

Table 2.11 brings together, for India, estimates of alternative measures of underemployment during the survey year 1993-94. These estimates are separately available by gender and by rural-urban location. A key result is that, all the estimates of the alternative measures are *lower* than the prevalence rates estimated by reference to hours/days worked during the reference week. Thus, as against the estimate of 18 per cent underemployment (in terms of working less than 40 hours per week) for rural India, less than 3 per cent of weekly status workforce are reported to be seeking or available for work according to daily status. The corresponding figures for urban India are 9 per cent (on the 40-hour week criterion) and less than 2 per cent (on seeking or available for work in daily status) among those classified as workers by current weekly status.

It is possible that significantly lower estimates of unemployment (as reported by the respondents themselves) amongst those classified as workers (on the priority rule) on the basis of current weekly status may be conditioned by perceived lack of work opportunities. However as noted earlier, given the absence of paid weekly off-days or the provision for medical leave, the possibility of a good proportion of those working less than five days a week being genuinely not available for work (and hence outside the labour force) should not be discounted.

Another key facet of the structure of employment is the distinction between the formal or organized segment and the informal or unorganized segment. While modern technology embodied in equipment produced by machine made or electronic machine tools provides the basis of high labour productivity in the formal sector, in employment data it becomes necessary to approximate productivity by reference to associated or concomitant characteristics such as legal protection to workers, stability of employment status, large size in terms of the number of workers employed, public ownership or corporate status and so on. In so far as a range of protective and beneficial labour legislation is available only to the workers in the formal sector, the proportion of such workers is also an indicator of the quality of employment.

In India, the Ministry of Labour compiles labour data. Annual figures on employment in non-agricultural establishments employing 10 or more workers in the public and private sectors are published. In addition, data are also published on employment in units covered by a range of protective labour legislations. Some examples are, the Plantation Labour Act (1951), the Mines Act (1952), the Factories Act (1948) and the Shops and Establishments Act. The Annual Survey of Industries collects data on Employment in respect of units covered by the Factories Act under the collection of Statistics Act (1953). By putting together the data from these sources, and, for any broad industry group, selecting the data source, which yields a higher estimate of employment, we can get an estimate of formal segment employment from the perspective of legislative protection to the workforce.

Informal sector employment, from this perspective of legislative protection, is derived as a *residual* by deducting formal segment employment from total employment by industry groups estimated from the employment-unemployment surveys. This residual approach is to be preferred to the direct estimates of employment in establishments below a certain size (typically defined by reference to number of workers). This follows from the fact that, in a situation where the labour force and employment statuses frequently change for persons who are not regular employees especially in household enterprises, establishment-based enquiries (such as the economic census or special small enterprise surveys) cannot capture the volume of employment properly. For a contrasting view, see the recent ILO-SAAT study on Pakistan (ILO-SAAT,1997).

Table 2.12 presents estimates of the share of the informal segment in the workforce in the major Industry Divisions for India (for rural and urban areas put together) for 1972-73, 1987-88 and 1993-94. A set of estimates for the urban workforce in Pakistan for 1972-73 and 1985-86 available in a recent research paper by Burki and Afaqi (1996) is also presented in the same table.

It is seen that, taking all industry divisions together, the share of the informal sector in India is over 90 per cent. Even if we restrict our focus to the non-agricultural sector, by 1993-94, the share of the informal sector had risen to over 76 per cent from about 65 per cent in 1972-73. The estimates for urban Pakistan also show a rise in the share of the informal sector from 69 per cent in 1972-73 to 73 per cent in 1985-86. It is seen from the above that the proportion of the workforce at least formally covered by legal protection (minimum labour standards) is not more than 10 per cent in India. Even if we restrict ourselves to the non-agricultural sector, the formal segment is only about 25 per cent.

In Pakistan, where the share of the formal segment in the *urban* workforce is little over 27 per cent, the share of the formal sector in the total workforce is not likely to be much larger than in India if we allow for the continued dominance of agriculture and allied activities (which is almost entirely in the informal sector) in the industrial distribution of the total (rural plus urban) workforce.

In India, another aspect of the formal sector employment is the dominance of the public sector. Currently, the share of the public sector (covering the Central and State Governments and local bodies besides the departmental and non-departmental commercial undertakings) in total formal sector employment is 62 per cent.

Viewed from a different perspective, a key feature of employment in the formal sector is the stability of employment measured in terms of regular flow of wage/salary income. This facet of the quality of employment can be captured by identifying employees (in the status-wise classification of the workforce) who are "regular wage and salaried workers". Such a classification is available for India in the quinquennial Employment-Unemployment Surveys (conducted since 1972-73). In 1993-94, the proportion of the total workforce classified as 'regular wage and salaried workers' was a little under 14 per cent and as a proportion of the employees, the share of this segment was 30 per cent.

In the other countries of South Asia, the data on employment status do not offer a break-up of employees as regular wage and salaried workers on the one hand and casual (daily-wage) labour (see Table 2.13). In Pakistan, where about 32 per cent of the workforce is classified as 'employees', the proportion of regular wage and salaried workers among employees in the total workforce is about 10 per cent. In Nepal (with 21 per cent of workforce classified as employees) and Bangladesh (12 per cent), the share of regular wage and salaried workers among total employees may be less than 30 per cent. Taking the share to be, roughly, 25 per cent, the regular wage and salaried workers would form between 3 to 5 per cent of the total workforce.

In the case of Sri Lanka, where 61 per cent of the workforce is classified as 'employees', we have a break-up of workers as those in the public sector and the rest as employees in the private sector. It is seen that from a level of close to 20 per cent in 1990 the share of public sector employees in the workforce has fallen to 15 per cent now (1996). A recent census of public sector employees in Sri Lanka (for 1994) shows that about 18 per cent (those not having the facility of paid leave-of-absence from work) belong to the category of temporary workers, apprentices, etc. Unlike in other countries of South Asia, a much larger proportion (more than 30 per cent) of the employees in the private sector fall in the category of regular wage and salaried workers. This follows from the large presence of plantations in the industry group 'agriculture and allied activities' and the sizeable share of the high productivity services sector in the industrial distribution of the Sri Lankan workforce.

Plantation workers in Sri Lanka, even if they are not regular wage and salaried workers are covered by a range of protective labour legislation, including, in particular, minimum wage legislation. In this context, it is worth noting that real wages in this sector have risen significantly, especially since the mid-eighties.

In contrast to the regular wage and salaried workers, the usual labourers, the numerically dominant among those classified as employees, experience a high degree of open unemployment during the year. However, such workers, especially if employed in the agricultural sector are formally covered by Minimum Wage regulations. Here again, as in the case of agricultural workers in Sri Lanka, real wage rates have risen since the mid-seventies.

Clearly, employers, own-account workers and unpaid family workers, who together constitute the category of self-employed workers, are not covered by any labour laws and belong to the informal sector. The proportion of the workforce belonging to the category of the self-employed, therefore, defines a lower-bound estimate of the share of the informal sector in total employment. On this approximation, at least 88 per cent of the workforce in Bangladesh, 78 per cent in Nepal, 67 per cent in Pakistan, and 54 per cent in India belong to the informal sector. At 40 per cent, this proportion is the lowest in Sri Lanka.

2.6 Unemployment and Characteristics of the Unemployed

Despite widespread scepticism about the usefulness of the concept of unemployment, a better understanding of the relationship between poverty and unemployment (supplemented by an analysis of underemployment of the employed population) is essential for the design of labour and employment policies in South Asia.

The status distribution of the workforce discussed in the preceding paragraphs is also important from the perspective of understanding unemployment and underemployment. Indian data show the incidence of open unemployment by current weekly or current daily status to be systematically higher for those classified as casual labourers on usual status than for the self-employed. Data for Pakistan (for 1982-83) show the prevalence of underemployment among unpaid family workers to be the highest (close to 26 per cent) and the least among those classified as employees on current (weekly) status.

Given this broad association, the rising share of employees, especially if they belong to the category of casual labourers, and a reduction in the share of the self-employed witnessed in all the countries of South Asia, would, *ceteris paribus*, tend to push up the rates of open unemployment. Has this happened?

Evidence on unemployment rates (as a proportion of those in the labour force) during the reference week, as also on the daily status for India, are presented for two points of time by gender and rural-urban location in Table 2.14. It is seen that, in Bangladesh, India and Sri Lanka, the unemployment rates have *fallen* over the two periods in almost all segments, with the exception of females in urban India.

In Pakistan, the unemployment rates for males in 1994-95 was the same as that for 1986-87. The unemployment rates for females show a sharp rise over the same period. However, as noted earlier, there has been an important change in the concepts used. Also, given the very low labour force participation rates for women in Pakistan, high unemployment rates (as a percentage of the labour force) do not indicate a high proportion of women being unemployed.

Nepal provides the other exception to the common experience of India and Bangladesh in that, between 1984-85 and 1995-96, unemployment rates for persons in both rural and urban Nepal as well as in the country as a whole show an increase. However, as noted earlier, against the backdrop of the rising share of employees, it is the experience of India and Bangladesh and (for males) in Pakistan as well, that is contrary to expectations.

Table 2.15 presents a distribution of the unemployed during the week by duration of unemployment (by level of education and gender) for Pakistan and Sri Lanka.

There are significant contrasts between the two countries, and, within Sri Lanka, between males and females. In Pakistan, close to 60 per cent of the currently unemployed had been unemployed for less than six months, and, nearly two-fifth had been unemployed for less than one month. In contrast, an overwhelming proportion of the unemployed in Sri Lanka had been unemployed for more than six months, with nearly 75 per cent of the unemployed experiencing a spell of unemployment exceeding 12 months. A larger proportion of females than males had been unemployed for more than one year (80 instead of 67 per cent). Significantly, shorter spells of unemployment in Pakistan go together with a majority of the unemployed being illiterate and a much smaller proportion of the unemployed having 'matric and above' level of education than in Sri Lanka. In Pakistan, while a majority of those unemployed for less than one month are those with previous work experience, among those unemployed for larger spells (1 to 6 months, and 6 months and over) a majority were new entrants to the labour force without previous work experience. Similarly, the larger share of the longer duration unemployed among women (compared to men) in Sri Lanka is to be seen in the context of a much larger proportion (55 per cent compared to 34 per cent) of them having GCE-O level and above education. Clearly, larger spells of unemployment are associated with the aspirations of the educated unemployed and the job-availability situation and their willingness/ability to wait for jobs of their choice.

For India, we now have tabulations for the 15-19 age groups (50th Round of the NSS Employment-Unemployment Survey, 1993-94) based on some key characteristics of those who were unemployed on *all* the seven days during the reference week. These are available separately by gender and by rural-urban location. The relevant estimates have been brought together in Table 2.16.

Focusing first on the duration of the current spell of unemployment, the proportion of those unemployed for more than six months in India is closer to the Sri Lankan situation - especially for urban males and urban females. Also, as in the case of Sri Lanka, the proportion of unemployed having below secondary level of education is lower (compared to their rural counterparts).

Tied to this is the fact that an overwhelming proportion of the urban unemployed (again more so for urban females than for urban males) sought full-time regular wage/salaried work in non-agriculture. The higher proportion of unemployed with a duration of unemployment greater than six months for rural males than for rural females is to be seen in the context of a larger proportion of the unemployed rural males (relative to the unemployed rural females) seeking full-time regular wage/salaried jobs in non-agricultural activities.

The substantial share of youth (15-24 years) among those unemployed on all the seven days of the reference week is consistent with the fact that a majority of them are new entrants to the labour force. Even in the case of rural females, the fact that only 42 per cent of the unemployed are new entrants to the labour force is consistent with the fact that the share of the youth is 44 per cent, compared to the much higher share of youth among the unemployed in the case of rural males and both urban males and urban females.

To design and implement policy to combat the problem of unemployment, further analysis of the unemployed along several other dimensions would be necessary. First, there is the spatial or (sub-national) regional dimension. For India, the quinquennial employment-unemployment surveys since 1972-73 make it possible to generate unemployment estimates on usual, weekly and daily status, separately for males and females and for the rural-urban segments according to NSS regions, with each region comprising two or more districts constructed to yield, to the extent possible, a homogeneous representation of the agro-climatic zone below the level of the states. In the NSS 50th Round (1993-94) survey, employment-unemployment data is also available for 18 cities, each with a population of 1 million and above and three sub-classes of towns with population less than 50,000; between 50,000 and 200,000; and 200,000 to 1 million.

In Sri Lanka, we have a provincial profile of the labour force for 1993, which provides estimates of employment and unemployment for seven provinces of Sri Lanka, separately by gender. In Nepal, we have separate estimates for three broad regions: mountains, hills, and the *terai*. It is seen that the reported rates of unemployment, for both males and females, are the highest in the *terai* region (see ILO-SAAT, 1997).

India also has estimates of unemployment by household type classified by principal means of livelihood; principal household industry (at the one digit level); size class of land cultivated (rural areas); and separately for the scheduled castes and scheduled tribes.

It must be stressed that despite the availability of sub-national estimates and estimates of a number of characteristics of unemployment, these details can at best help in the design of policy and for broad targeting. However, both for implementation of specific programmes and monitoring of these programmes, sample surveys conducted on a national basis are not much help. For that, we would require local surveys on a complete enumeration basis for programme implementation, and sample surveys with a control segment for monitoring purposes.

2.7 Labour Force Characteristics of Children, Youth and Women

2.7.1 Child Labour

The presence in the workforce/labour force of a proportion of children below 15 years of age, is often a negative indicator of living standards as it implies rejection of the socially desirable alternative of attending school. Even when the labour participation of this age group is combined with schooling, as is the case of 10 to 20 per cent of the children in the workforce in India, participation in the workforce is perceived as a negative indicator of living standards. The freedom of a school-going child to spend his/her after-school hours or vacations as (s)he wishes is seen as a positive value.

Table 2.17 brings together the estimates of workforce/labour force participation rates among children in South Asia. As noted earlier, except in India, children in the workforce/labour force belong to the 10-14 years age group. Labour force participation rates among children are the lowest in Sri Lanka, and the highest in Nepal. The LFPRs are roughly the same in India and Pakistan, though children (10-14 years) in Pakistan are a slightly larger proportion of the workforce than children (5-14 years) in India.

Invaluable information on children (5-14 years) in the labour force are available from the tabulations in the NSS 50th Round survey (1993-94) for India. These are provided separately for boys and girls and rural-urban locations (see Table 2.18).

A classification of such workers by school attendance status shows that an overwhelming proportion of them had dropped out of school. It is, however, difficult to tell whether participation in work followed or caused the dropping out. Another key characteristic of child labourers is that while in rural India they are primarily engaged in household enterprises, in urban India, a majority of them work as hired labour. Close to 61 per cent of the working children reported "supplementing household income" as the reason for being in the workforce, with a further 20 per cent (in rural India) citing "labour shortage in household enterprises" as the reason. It is significant that while about 10 per cent of the urban boys report the "acquisition of skills" as the reason for working, the proportion of such children is only 3 per cent among rural boys and girls and 1 per cent for urban girls.

2.7.2 Youth

Our discussion on unemployment in the countries of South Asia highlighted the high share of youth (age group 15-24 years) among the unemployed, many of whom were new entrants to the labour force. Table 2.19 brings together available data on some of the key labour force characteristics of youth in South Asia.

In Bangladesh, unemployment rates reported for youth are higher than those for the total population. Reflecting the same phenomenon, in both India and Sri Lanka the share of youth in the total unemployed population is higher than their share in population. The other point of interest is that in India, as we shift from usual status to weekly and currently daily status, the share of youth in total unemployment goes down. A common result is that, over time, there has been a decline in the LFPR among youth, reflecting greater participation in education. If this trend persists, it will moderate the labour force boom that is expected to occur in most countries of the region following the slow down in growth of population and the consequential shift in age structure towards the prime working age groups.

2.7.3 Women

' Finally, we note some key characteristics of women in the labour force in South Asia (Table 2.20). As stated earlier, in all the countries of the region, the reported workforce participation rates are lower and unemployment rates are higher for women than men. This is particularly true for Pakistan. Even in Bangladesh, prior to the adoption of a more inclusive concept of work, the reported participation rates were almost as low as those currently reported for Pakistan. In part, therefore, the extremely low participation rates reported for women in Pakistan may reflect the inability of the existing labour force surveys to adequately capture women's participation in economic activity. It would be necessary to use a more inclusive concept of economic activity, and, therefore, of work, which is in consonance with the concept and definitions adopted by the UN System of National Accounts (1993), so that the measurement of the workforce is in tune with the concepts and definitions used for the measurement of national income.

The low levels of workforce participation rates of women in the countries of South Asia must be seen in conjunction with the high levels of fertility that characterize these countries. The burden of child-bearing and child-rearing that they impose on women limits their ability to undertake the *additional* burden of participation in economic activity.

From the perspective of employment policy, the very high rates of open unemployment among women, especially in Sri Lanka, need to be addressed urgently.

As far as the quality of women's employment is concerned, the heavy concentration of women workers in the low productivity agriculture and allied activities sector in the countries of South Asia (with the exception of Sri Lanka); the dominance of self-employed (largely as unpaid family labour) with no legislative protection, and, among employees, the generally lower wages that women command compared to men, are major areas of concern.

2.8 Conclusion

Our review of the different facets of the size and structure of employment and unemployment in South Asia have brought to the fore some positive developments as well as some key areas of concern in South Asia.

♦ The decline in the share of the low productivity agricultural sector in the workforce; and, the rising levels of real product per worker in all the sectors of the economy (which translates into rising real wage rates in both the organized and the unorganized segments of the workforce) have been among the positive developments common to all the countries of South Asia.

♦ The high levels of illiteracy among workers, with the proportion of illiterate women workers close to or above 75 per cent; very high rates of underemployment in Nepal (47 per cent) and Sri Lanka (34 per cent) among those classified as workers; an overwhelming proportion of the workforce being located in the generally low productivity unorganized sector with little or no protective cover in terms of welfare benefits and job security (with Sri Lanka as a possible exception); the continued presence of children in the workforce with high (12 per cent) to very high (36 per cent) participation rates in India and Nepal; and the dominance of 'unpaid' family labour and the generally lower wages commanded by women in the workforce, are among the areas of concern.

♦ However, notwithstanding the importance of the areas of concern just noted, the observed pattern of labour absorption, and especially in Sri Lanka, the high rates of open unemployment (11 per cent of the labour force), are by far the most important employment issues confronting policy planners in South Asia.

♦ With regard to relative labour productivities, in most countries of South Asia, the agriculture (and allied activities) sector has had to absorb labour at a rate faster than the GDP originating in that sector, with the result that the index of relative productivity has declined further over time. Significantly, it is not the only sector that has had to play the role of a residual absorber of the expanding labour force.

The unregistered manufacturing sector in India, the construction sector in Pakistan and the 'other services' sector in Sri Lanka, with less than average levels of productivity per worker, have had to absorb an increasing share of the expanding workforce at a rate much faster than the expansion of value added in these sectors.

◆ The key factor underlying the pattern of labour absorption has been the failure of the high productivity organized sector to absorb, at an adequate pace, the expanding labour force. This, in turn, is a consequence of both a low pace of growth of value added in this sector and a failure to absorb labour force even at this rate. A rise in the share of the registered manufacturing sector in India in total GDP from 10 per cent to 13.6 per cent was accompanied by a small *decline* in the already small share of the sector in the workforce (from 2.3 to 2.1 per cent).

◆ The pattern of low absorption of the workforce in the organized sectors of the economy on the one hand, and the generally low pace of growth on the other, has focused the attention of policy planners on issues of labour market flexibility and the extent of 'outward' orientation of the economy. While the lack of labour market flexibility is seen as a factor responsible for the failure of the high productivity sectors to absorb labour even in proportion to the expansion in value added, the low pace of overall growth is attributed to the so-called 'inward' looking strategies of industrialization. Whether and to what extent these perceptions are based on the ground realities in the countries of South Asia are examined in Chapters 3 and 4.

3 Labour Market Institutions and Labour Market Flexibility

Conceptual issues related to labour market flexibility are significant because of the link they have with employment generation. In broad terms the process of economic reforms that all the countries of South Asia have embarked upon in varying degrees is essentially intended to restore flexibility to markets. State interventions in labour markets have served to promote employment and improve the quality of employment. Insofar as employment promotion is concerned these have taken the form of direct employment programmes, primarily in rural areas, promotional and protective policies for small industries and the expansion of the public sector. These were augmented by a number of regulatory and legislative interventions designed to improve the quality of employment by providing standards for workplace safety, increasing job and employment security, regulating the framework for wage determination and wage payments and a variety of pecuniary and non-pecuniary benefits. In this section we will address this latter class of, regulatory and legislative interventions and examine their link with labour market flexibility.

3.1 Adherence to ILO Conventions

With the exception of Nepal, South Asian countries have a long tradition of protective legislation and labour standards. One measure of the extent of these protections is the adherence of these countries to basic human rights principles, as expressed by their adherence to ILO Conventions and Recommendations. Once ratified conventions create binding obligations; even in the absence of ratification, they serve as a standard of reference for national law and practice. While these conventions cover a variety of circumstances, seven of these have been categorized as fundamental human rights conventions. These are:

Forced Labour Convention, 1930 (No. 29) : Requires the suppression of forced or compulsory labour in all its forms. Certain exceptions are permitted, such as military service, convict labour properly supervised, emergencies such as wars, fires, earthquakes, etc.

Freedom of Association and Protection of the Right to Organize Convention, 1948 (No. 87): Establishes the right of all workers and employers to form and join organizations of their own choosing without prior authorization, and lays down a series of guarantees for the free functioning of organizations without interference by the public authorities.

Right to Organize and Collective Bargaining Convention, 1949 (No. 98): Provides for protection against anti-union discrimination, for protection of workers' and employers' organizations against acts of interference by each other, and for measures to promote collective bargaining.

Abolition of Forced Labour Convention, 1957 (No. 105): Prohibits the use of any form of forced or compulsory labour as a means of political coercion or education, punishment for the expression of political or ideological views, workforce mobilization, labour discipline, punishment for participation in strikes, or discrimination.

Equal Remuneration Convention, 1951 (No. 100) : Calls for equal pay for men and women for work of equal value.

Discrimination (Employment and Occupation) Convention, 1958 (No. 111): Calls for a national policy to eliminate discrimination in access to employment, training and working conditions, on grounds of race, colour, sex, religion, political opinion, national extraction or social origin and to promote equality of opportunity and treatment.

Minimum Age Convention, 1973 (No. 138) :Aims at the abolition of child labour, stipulating that the minimum age for admission to employment shall not be less than the age of completion of compulsory schooling.

South Asian countries have on the whole a good record of respecting and ratifying ILO Conventions. As is seen from Table 3.1 except for the Child Labour Convention, South Asian countries have in fact ratified most of these conventions. Non-ratification of a convention in itself does not imply absence of rights. India for instance has not ratified the conventions on Free Association and Collective Bargaining. The Indian Constitution and laws however guarantee freedom of association and their provisions are enforceable and protected by the Indian judicial system. Conversely, periods of national emergency and/or martial law rule have led to the suspension of these basic rights. All South Asian countries have been through these phases. The period beginning 1990 has seen the restoration of multi-party democracy in all these countries.

Table 3. 1: ILO Conventions in Force in South Asia

	Bangladesh*	India	Nepal	Pakistan	Sri Lanka
Total Number Of Conventions Ratified	33	35	7	31	31
Key Human Rights Conventions:	Date of Joining:				
29. Forced Labour	22.06.72	30.11.54		23.12.57	05.04.50
87. Freedom of Association and Protection of the Right to Organize	22.06.72			14.02.51	15.09.95
98. Right to Organize And Collective Bargaining	22.06.72		11.11.96	26.05.52	13.12.72
100. Equal Remuneration	28.01.98	25.09.58	10.06.76		01.04.93
105. Abolition Of Forced Labour	22.06.72			15.02.60	
111. Discrimination (Employment And Occupation)	22.06.72	03.06.60	19.09.74	24.01.61	
138. Minimum Age			30.05.97		
Priority Conventions					
81. Labour Inspection	22.06.72	07.04.49		10.10.53	03.04.56
122. Employment Policy					
129.Labour Inspection (Agriculture)					
144. Tripartite Consultation (International Labour Standard)	17.04.79	27.02.78	21.03.95	25.10.94	17.03.94

* In the case of Bangladesh the Conventions were often in force earlier due to their application to (the then) undivided Pakistan.

In some cases non-ratification is due to problems related to implementation. For example, the ILO has identified certain conventions as being critical for the implementation of employment policies. In particular, those related to labour inspection in agriculture and employment policy would be difficult to implement given the extent of self-employment and family labour in the unorganized and rural sectors of these economies. Agricultural inspection would be difficult to implement in a structure characterized by widely dispersed small holding cultivation. Where labour is used in more organized settings such as in plantations, both India and Sri Lanka have in fact ratified the conventions.

Bangladesh, India, Pakistan and Sri Lanka have created a fairly extensive framework of legal protection for workers. Some of these laws date back to their colonial past but the others have evolved in the course of their development experience. The key elements of this framework are outlined below.

3.2 Legal Protection for Workers in South Asia

3.2.1 India[1]

Indian labour jurisprudence has evolved from its colonial heritage and the requirements of social security and welfare have carried over to the post-independence era. As part of the developments in labour legislation and workers rights in Britain and the trade union movement in India, the colonial Government had enacted some key protective legislations such as the Payment of Wages Act and the (registration of) Trade Unions Act. The requirements of the war effort led to the formulation of the Defence of India Rules which were the precursor to a number of post-independence economic and regulatory laws namely the Industrial Disputes Act and the Industrial Development and Regulation Act. After Independence, labour legislation came under the purview of both the Union and Concurrent lists, leading to both state and central legislation on the subject. This has led to considerable inter-state variation in definitions and coverage. In addition the number of labour laws in both the centre and the states have increased over a period of time starting from the Trade Unions Act in 1926 to the Public Liability Insurance Act in 1991. In just the central sphere alone there are as many as 47 different acts covering different aspects of labour policy. A common feature of most of these laws is that coverage is usually restricted to size of establishment. The most common restrictions are applicable to establishments, under the Factories Act, which employ 10 or more workers and use power, or to 20 or more workers without the use of power.

The individual contract of employment is governed largely by the provisions of the Industrial Employment Standing Orders Act (1948) and

---

1. See the discussion in Venkatratnam (1997); Johri (1997); and ILO-SAAT (1996).

the Industrial Disputes (IDA) Act (1948). In addition judicial pronouncements have had a profound impact on the interpretation of the conditions under which a worker could be separated from his job. In a series of judicial decisions[2] the courts have narrowed the scope of termination from service. As a consequence, ordinary termination is now virtually limited to cases of proven misconduct, which have been outlined in the Standing Orders and require elaborate domestic enquiries before being implemented. These domestic enquiries take on extremely rigid forms and must adhere to formal court procedures. All other separations are deemed to be retrenchments. Further, Standing Orders are mandatory for all organizations with 100 or more workers (50 or more in some states). Such units are usually required to adhere closely to the model Standing Orders formulated by the state. They vary from state to state and specify job security by specifying classification of employee categories and conditions for termination. Employee Classifications can be changed only by changing the Standing Orders and that would require the consent of all the workers[3]. The resulting freezing of job roles into a rigid classification makes it difficult for employers to re-deploy workforce without prolonged negotiations.[4] Income security is ensured by provisions for timely payments of wages/salaries and methods of computation of hours worked.

Employment security is provided through regulation of layoffs,[5] retrenchments and closure by specifying conditions governed by the ID Act. The characteristic provisions of these are that no retrenchment or closure can take place in designated establishments (employing more than 100 workers) without prior permission from the state.

Most of these rules and regulations for improving quality of employment primarily govern large industrial establishments employing more than 100 workers and thus create a barrier to exploiting scale economies in the private sector. The cost at the margin of crossing the threshold limit can be quite high and would deter expansion of existing plants. In so far as new investment is concerned it increases the incentive to adopt labour saving technology. In

---

2. Chandulal v. Management of Pan American Airways, SC 1985; or Central Inland Water Transport Corporation v. Brojo Nath Ganguly and Others, SC 1986

3. In the absence of a recognized worker representative, the requirement of consent can become one of consensus amongst all unions and groups.

4. In the public sector, these have the perverse implication that the introduction of computers which usually reduces job categories ends up increasing it in India by the creation of the ubiquitous "Computer Operator".

5. Termination refers to the simple separation of an individual from his job. As against this retrenchment and layoffs are both autonomous reduction of workers in specified categories or all categories in response to changes in production conditions or demands. Retrenchment is permanent while layoffs are temporary or seasonal in nature. Both operate on a last in first out principle.

the public sector these have added an additional dimension of inflexibility to managements already constrained by an excessively centralized political control.[6] In addition to these rules and regulations limited protection primarily covering working hours, holidays, etc. is provided to employees in other establishments through the operation of the various Shops and Commercial Establishments Act as modified in different states

The experience of the last two decades has shown that technological progress makes earlier job classifications obsolete. For example, in a paper-based office system, filing, typing, secretarial, accounts and executive tasks could be said to require different personnel. The advent of computers and multi-tasking has implied a unification of these different tasks into more compact result oriented categories. For an enterprise to take advantage of this, it would need to implement on-the-job training and greater rewards to those workers exhibiting greater flexibility and ability to adapt. In ideal circumstances these types of changes would have been possible in the framework of enterprise or industry level collective bargaining. As we shall see later both the legal structure and the mechanism of government intervention is rather inadequate in this critical dimension.

The process of dispute resolution in India is described by the Industrial Disputes Act, 1947 which in turn follows the structure of the Defence of India Rules. Under these rules, and the later Act, the state is a necessary party in any settlement or dispute resolution. In the event of a dispute the concerned state governments appoint a conciliation officer, who reports on the dispute. Thereafter it is for the government to act on that report or refer the matter to the appropriate tribunal for adjudication and settlement. While one can see the logic for the state retaining the right to intervene in industrial disputes, the essential inclusion of the state in order to refer the dispute to the various tribunals has unnecessarily complicated the process of dispute settlement. Further since the state is an essential participant in the process, parties to the dispute can challenge the actions of the state via the writ jurisdiction of the High Courts. So the state which was initially not a party to the dispute now becomes a central actor in the delayed resolution of any dispute. Further at the time when these laws were formulated the State was a small employer, but with the growth of the public sector the State has emerged as the dominant employer in the organized sector, accounting for nearly 19 million of the almost 27 million organized sector employees. In such a situation from being an impartial outside intermediary the state has

---

6. The introduction of computers in banking has been limited by agreements which specify the number of vouchers that will be processed and the number and type of machines that will be introduced.

become an involved and potentially non-neutral "insider". Its actions and decisions have to be taken keeping in mind their repercussions for the vast public sector workforce.

Though in several places of the Industrial Disputes Act and associated rules the term 'recognized' union has been mentioned, at no place does it get defined or explained. The Trade Union Act merely provides for registration of any group of seven workers as a union. The outcome of this is to create a multiplicity of trade unions in any industry impeding the ability of the employer to effectively negotiate. The multiplicity of trade unions and their association with different political groups has weakened the process of collective bargaining in India. Further under Section 18(1) of the Industrial Disputes Act, 1947 any bilateral settlement entered into between the management and the workers is binding only on the signatories to the settlement, thus only on members of the concerned union. Some states, namely, Maharashtra, and Orissa have, however, formulated rules to recognize unions.

In addition to laws on the terms of employment there are numerous laws on health and safety standards and a variety of pecuniary and non-pecuniary benefits to workers. These govern issues of workplace environment, working conditions and hours of work. Under the Factories Act, no adult worker is allowed to work for more than 48 hours in any week. The Employees State Insurance Act, 1948, provides for certain benefits to employees, such as sickness, medical, maternity, disablement, dependent and funeral allowances. In addition pension benefits accrue to employees of Government departments and industries in the public sector and some private sector industries. The Payment of Bonus Act, 1965 provides for the payment of bonus and requires that the minimum bonus payable to an employee should not be less than 8.33 per cent of the wages earned by him during the accounting year. In addition various Acts have been legislated to meet specific situations pertaining to labour. These include enactments like the Dangerous Machines (Regulation) Act, Employers Liability Act, Fatal Accidents Act, and Payment of Gratuity Act.

Minimum wages are covered under The Minimum Wages Act (MWA) (1948). The Act schedules jobs or employment categories where minimum wages are to be made obligatory. These scheduled jobs pertain to "sweated labour" or jobs where there is a higher likelihood of "exploitation of labour". The activities cover industries, mines, quarries and agriculture. The act covers any employer who employs, directly or indirectly, one or more employees in any of the scheduled employments defined in the Act. The scope of the MWA is thus very wide and includes all employers. The act however only refers to employment in the scheduled categories, starting with 13 employment categories (Agriculture and 12 others), but there has been a steady expansion in the list. At present the number of protected job categories range from 79 in the state of Orissa to 8 in Manipur.[7]

The 15th Indian Labour Conference[8] (1957) introduced the idea of the need-based minimum wage. This resolution, like in the Committee on Fair Wages recommended that the standard working class family should be taken to comprise three consumption units for one earner, the earnings of women, children and adolescents being disregarded. Further it recommended that in assessing needs, the following factors should be taken into account:

(i)   the minimum food requirements should be calculated on the basis of a net intake of 2,700 calories for an average Indian adult of moderate activity;

(ii) clothing requirements should be estimated at a per capita consumption of 18 yards per annum, that would give for the average worker's family of four, a total of 72 yards;

(iii) in respect of housing, the norm should be the minimum rent charged by Government in any area of houses provided under Subsidized Industrial Housing Scheme for low income groups; and,

(iv) fuel, lighting and other miscellaneous items should constitute 20 per cent of the total minimum wage.

While these norms have been accepted, endorsed by the courts and effectively implemented for organized sector workers this has not been the case with minimum wages applicable for unorganized labour. An analysis of the data[9] on minimum wages shows differences in the statutory minimum wage across states, which is understandable if we allow for differences in cost of living, but also across occupations in a given state. This latter difference is partly due to differences in the labour requirement in different jobs but partly also due to political economy and considerations related to employer's ability to pay. This pattern also reveals a curious dichotomy in the attitude of the courts. In a case in 1958 relating to wage fixation, the court[10] held ability to pay as not a relevant issue; what is considered relevant in fixing minimum wages is the wage required by the employee to survive.

7. Anant and Sundaram (1995); also see ILO-SAAT (1996), Chapter 2.
8. The Indian Labour Conference is a tripartite forum with representatives from unions, employer associations and the state.
9. Anant and Sundaram (1995).
10. United Salt Works & Industries v. Workmen, SC (1962) 1 LLJ 3; also Crown Aluminium Works v. Workmen AIR 1958, SC 30.

However, elsewhere[11] the court also accepted the legitimacy of the industry cum region as the relevant standard to fix wages. A comparison of the wages prevailing in 1960 (or at first fixation at 1960 prices) and at the point of last revision (converted to 1960 prices using the CPI for industrial workers) shows the latter to be higher in real terms in almost all cases. However this finding must be tempered by the fact of low absolute levels of these minimum wages. By some calculations[12] the poverty line wage would be more than the statutory minimum wage in some states. This is both due to low levels of the wage and its infrequent revision. Further till the 1980s most states had no provision for inflation indexation which, combined with long gaps between revisions, implied spells of declining real minimum wages.

Wages outside the informal sector are covered by the institutionalized processes of the periodic Pay Commissions and wage settlements under the aegis of the Bureau of Public Enterprises for the public sector and Wage Boards and Collective Bargaining in the private sector. We have already noted the impediments to collective bargaining in the legal framework. A consequence of this is seen in the data on strikes and lockouts (Tables 3.2 and 3.3). The number of workers involved in strikes and lockouts in India is almost ten times that in any other South Asian country, which is significantly higher than the corresponding sizes of the workforce or organized workforce. In the public sector where wage determination has superficial elements of bi-partite negotiation there is little scope for agreements, which link wage awards to measures to enhance productivity. The concern is rather to see "how much more we can get" partly as a response to the perceived political strength of the state. The private sector has seen a variety of experiments to get over the limitations of the legal framework. In 1958 the Indian Labour Conference evolved the concepts of "code of conduct" and "joint management councils" but by the mid 1960s both had been reduced to purely notional concepts. In 1957 the recommendations of the Indian Labour Conference led to the formation of non-statutory wage boards with the first wage board being set up in 1957 in cotton textiles, and 20 more set up in the seven years till 1965. The wage board would decide on the minimum wage for unskilled work in the industry and a structure of differentials for other employees. The procedures and decision making of both the board and the Government in implementing the awards grew gradually longer

---

11. Bijay Cotton Mills v. Workmen AIR 1960, SC 692 693.
12. See ILO-SAAT (1996) Ch. 2. Poverty line wages are calculated from the monthly poverty line expenditure per capita being earned by a single worker for a family of two dependants in 20 working days.

with it taking as much as five years in some cases. In view of this and also the politicization of these boards they lost favour and declined in importance; as a result only seven were set up in the next 25 years.

3.2.2 Pakistan[13]

Pakistan inherited a framework of protective legislation similar to India's from its colonial heritage. The subsequent developments in labour laws in Pakistan have mirrored the shifts in governance from martial law to democratic governance. A key feature of most of the protective legislation developed in Pakistan is that its domain of applicability is usually restricted to enterprises with 10 or more workers covered under the Factories Act (1934). Somewhat less restrictive support is extended to other units under the Shops and Establishments Ordinance (1969).

Individual employment relationships are governed by the laws relating to Compensation and Employment (Standing Orders). The 1960 Industrial and Commercial (Standing Orders) Ordinance codified the standing orders and extended them to all enterprises and the set of benefits available to all workers. As a result of this act, greater security was afforded to covered workers. Bonus was made a statutory entitlement linked to profit under the Companies Profit's Worker's Participation Act (1968). There are similarly other legislations providing for a variety of non-wage benefits to organized sector workers.

Individual and collective disputes and grievances have to be resolved through the collective bargaining procedure laid out in the Industrial Relations Ordinance (1969). The Ordinance covers all establishments employing 50 or more workers. Registered trade unions can become eligible to Collective Bargaining Agents (CBA) if they represent more than a third of the employees. If there is more than one such union then there is a provision for secret ballots. The CBA alone can raise disputes. The primary focus however is on a bilateral solution. If the bilateral process breaks down the state *may* appoint a conciliator and if that fails the state can refer the dispute to the labour court or commission, which is legally binding. However recourse to courts is not restricted and the state is not compelled to intervene. The employer's right to terminate employment either individually or for large groups is restricted in the case of enterprises covered under The Industrial Relations Ordinance, as all of these fall in the rubric of disputes and require the consent of the CBA.

Minimum wages are regulated under the West Pakistan Minimum Wages for Unskilled Workers Ordinance, 1969 and Minimum Wages

---

13. Chaudhry (n.d.); Khan (1997).

Ordinance, 1961. However, both of these cover all establishments, which employ 50 or more workers. The 1961 law provides for minimum wages in select industries. There is no explicit provision for minimum wages in the informal sector.

3.2.3 Bangladesh[14]

Bangladesh has a legal framework similar to that in Pakistan. As in Pakistan regime shifts between martial law and democratic rule have been important determinants of the rights to unionize and strike as well as to collective bargaining. The major Acts are Workmen's Compensation Act (1923), Factories Act (1965), Employment of Labour (Standing Orders) Act 1965, and the Industrial Relations Ordinance (1969). These laws cover classification of workers, determination of working conditions, procedures for dispute resolution and various ways of terminating employment. Apart from regulating the employment contracts there are legislations granting right to form unions, collective bargaining and conditions for registration of unions, a necessary requirement being that the union represents at least 30 per cent of the workers. The selection of the collective bargaining agent is also spelt out. Thus purely at a formal level the legislative framework appears adequate for worker protection and facilitating adjustment in the workforce. However, due to inadequacies of enforcement institutions, violations in labour laws remain pending in courts; as many as 60 per cent of all cases in 1992 were pending. Collective bargaining has not been as successful as the laws would expect because of weak information systems at the plant level for workers as also the politicization of the trade unions.[15]

The Minimum Wages (Ordinance), 1961 and the corresponding rules provide for minimum wages. They were not implemented until 1973. These, however, only provide for minimum wages in specified industries and do not cover all workers. Minimum wage boards for specified industries set minimum wages (in the private sector and usually on account of failure of collective bargaining). Minimum wages are usually specified for all categories of workers in the industry. Minimum Wage Boards have recommended minimum wages for 38 industries during the last 20 years. However, some of these awards have not been revised for long periods of time leading to a decline in the real wage. In 1992 the Industrial Workers Wages and Productivity Commission recommended that minimum wages should be set keeping in mind the calorific needs of a worker family of two adults and two children. Thus by 1993, extreme Poverty Level Income was Tk 324

---

14. Anderson, Hossain and Sahota (1991); Rehman (1994).
15. Rehman (1994).

per capita (or Tk 972 per family).[16] However in 1993 the minimum wage was Tk 950, marginally less than the norm. The position is likely to be worse in urban areas due to the higher cost of living. Wages other than minimum wages are set through collective bargaining in the private sector and the Wage Commissions in the public sector. But here the organizational weaknesses of the trade union system as well as the lack of adequate information on demand conditions and productivity at the establishment or shop floor level have led to unsatisfactory performance. The HIID study[17] finds little evidence of a rise in wages due to union activity as well as a limited effect on employment.

3.2.4 Sri Lanka[18]

Sri Lanka has a legal framework that grants workers the right to form unions and to engage in industrial action. The legal framework for dispute resolution is provided for in the Industrial Disputes Act of 1950. These provide the machinery for collective bargaining, arbitration and conciliation. There is also legislation to contain unfair termination. Dismissal on disciplinary grounds has to be justified to labour tribunals; all other forms of termination are covered by the Termination of Workers Act of 1971. Under the act, termination can either occur with the consent of the workmen or by an order of the Commissioner. The Act covers all establishments employing more than 15 workers. As in the discussion on India these provisions are often cited as major factors that reduce the ability of the enterprise to flexibly adapt itself to rapidly changing business conditions.[19] Disputes in Sri Lanka were settled primarily by conciliation and after 1977 by arbitration. In the entire period after 1977 only 19 disputes were referred to Industrial Courts as against 135 in 1959 alone.

Wage determination in the organized sector can take place either by collective bargaining or through the mechanism of tripartite wage boards and remuneration boards set up under the Shops and Establishments Act. There do not appear to be any objective criteria for determining minimum wages but rather to rely on the wages being paid currently as the base to effect some improvement.[20] The consideration of ability to pay has been an important component in the decisions of these boards. Further automatic indexation has been given up in favour of periodic adjustment which tends to give a saw-toothed pattern to real wage behaviour. Comparing minimum

---

16. Ibid.
17. Anderson, Hossain and Sahota (1991).
18. Rodrigo (1994).
19. Ibid.
20. Korale (1997).

wages to poverty line requirements[21] it may be noted that till 1975 the agricultural minimum wage could hardly meet one person's poverty level consumption needs. Even for both industry and agriculture the minimum wages were only about 2.3 times the per capita poverty line expenditures, well below the average notion of 3 to 4 dependants to each earner. The gap is presumably filled by non-wage options for the family or by some earners in higher wage jobs.

3.2.5 Nepal[22]

Prior to the onset of multi-party democracy in 1990 the framework of labour legislation was rather limited. Individual labour contracts were largely governed by the common law precepts of 'master and servant'. These were modified slightly by the Factory and Factory Workers Act of 1959. There were virtually no other labour laws till 1974 when a provision was made for bonus. Collective laws and the right for association came only after 1990. The major developments have been the accession of Nepal to some of the key human rights conventions of the ILO (see Table 3.1) and the enactment of the Labour Act, 1992 and the Trade Union Act, 1992. These acts cover all establishments employing 10 or more workers or employees. The use of formal dispute settlement mechanisms is weak and in fact overt conflict is replaced by a variety of covert conflicts and militancy. The industrial relations institutions being young have not yet gained wide acceptability.

Minimum wages in Nepal are governed by both the Factory and Factory Workers Act and the subsequent Labour Act as well by customary law where an employer is obliged to pay a worker no less than the prevailing wage in the area. The formal mechanisms for setting minimum wages cover all establishments under the Labour Act.

3.3 Legal Institutions and Flexibility

The framework of legal protection outlined above in addition to the basic rights of association and human dignity encompasses three broad dimensions: Health and Workplace Security, Income Security and Job and Employment Security. The issues of health and environment safety have been important aspects of labour policy and have usually been uncontroversial. The areas of concern relate to job and employment security and income security. As noted earlier job and employment security regulations create a network of restrictions that reduce the ability of the employer to

---

21. ILO-SAAT *(1995).*
22. Mathur (1993); ILO-SAAT (1997a).

adjust to changing market conditions. This by itself would not be a problem if there was a system of effective collective bargaining in place because employers could trade productivity enhancing changes with greater incomes and/or employment. Unfortunately, collective bargaining systems in South Asia have tended to be weak (except possibly in Sri Lanka). This has been due to two reasons: first, in India, the legal framework for union recognition has been rather poor and attempts at reform have been hampered by political considerations; second, the thin spread and low credibility of the Trade Union Movement. The tendency to fragment (India and Pakistan), resort to strikes (India), depend on political affiliation (India, Bangladesh, and Pakistan), and use violence (Bangladesh) have been cited as major factors that determine job and income security in South Asia. Political affiliation in itself is not bad and can in fact be the basis for a strong movement. But, "politicization, in a pejorative sense, as used in this context, refers to the use of trade unions for issues which have little to do with worker interests or for establishing compromises which do not serve or enhance the interest of workers."[23] In addition, a factor common to all countries has been the imperfect information at the establishment level making it difficult for workers to assess the implications of technological change.

A conventional response to such rigidities in labour use has been to keep establishment size small. This has a dual advantage as most labour laws do not apply to small enterprises, and at the same time small enterprises can avail of the benefit from other support and benefits offered to them. The major problem with this method is that it loses the benefits of returns to scale. Secondly, establishments resort to the use of contract labour. In India there is evidence that from the mid 1980s when the Industrial Disputes Act was strengthened, the use of contract labour has increased.

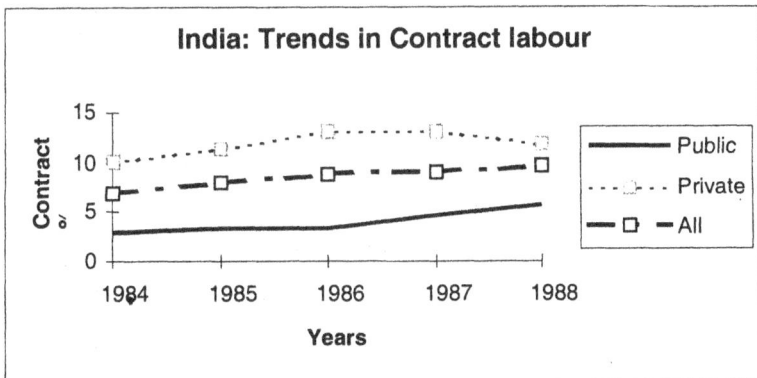

India: Trends in Contract labour

23. Rehman (1994).

While there is little direct evidence of these trends in the other countries, these trends are consistent with the increased growth in informal labour.

3.4 Wage Trends and Flexibility

Wages and labour cost are critical to our understanding of the concept of labour market flexibility. The link between wages and labour cost and flexibility has a number of dimensions. Firstly at the aggregate, all industry level, the concern is with whether changes in labour cost are consistent with the changes in productivity. In addition to consistency, wages and labour costs play a key role in providing incentives and allocative signals between industrial sectors and inside sectors and establishments between different jobs and occupations. We now turn to examine the evidence on these alternative dimensions.

In India, labour cost per person day measured at constant product prices has recorded significant growth[24] at around 4 per cent per annum between 1980 and 1993. Instead of measuring labour cost if we were to examine the behaviour in wage rates, then even these have seen a real rise with reference to the consumer price index. The growth in real wage rates has been of the order of 1.8 per cent (Table 3.4). There is limited data on composition of labour cost, but based on available data from the Annual Survey of Industries (ASI), it is seen that wages account for over 70 per cent to 80 per cent of total labour cost and there has been a marginal decline in the share of wages in total labour cost at the expense of the other components (welfare and retirement benefits). The public sector has a higher labour cost per day (Table 3.5). Further, in the public sector the share of wages and bonus in total labour cost is higher and the share of retirement benefits and staff welfare expenses is lower than that in the private sector. Taking all industries together the entire difference in labour cost between the public and private sectors is attributable to the differences in their respective wage costs. The wages in the informal sector as measured by agricultural wages seem to have risen faster than the wages in organized manufacturing (Tables 3.6 and 3.7). This is in part due to the slowing down of real wage growth in organized manufacturing in the late 1980s and 1990s. However in absolute levels the difference in wages between the two is quite significant.

In Pakistan real wages in the organized industrial sector have increased by approximately 4.8 per cent between 1980 and 1991; in contrast labour

24. The discussion in India and Pakistan is based on analysis of data for a sample of sectors covering final goods, key intermediates and capital goods. These cover agro-industries, textiles, chemicals, petro-products, basic metals and electrical and non-electrical machinery.

costs in the agricultural and informal sectors have grown at a much slower rate of only around 1 per cent in the same period. This is comparable to the results obtained in an earlier period[25] when both formal and informal sectors had seen a rise in real wages, but the rise in the formal sector was larger than that in the informal sector leading to a widening of the disparity between the two sectors. For workers in organized manufacturing the growth in wages has been accompanied by a striking reduction in the share of wages as compared to non-wage benefits. A recent study of the CMI data[26] reveals that wages have declined from 85 per cent of total remuneration to 67 per cent between 1970 and 1987. This decline was matched by a rise in the share of other cash benefits from 11.6 per cent to 23.6 per cent and in non-cash benefits from 3.22 per cent to 9.4 per cent. The growth in public sector wage has been somewhat less than that in the private sector[27] even though the absolute level of wages is higher in the public sector. This pattern is in contrast to India where the public sector has led the process of rise in labour cost.

An analysis of the labour cost data in India and Pakistan at the sectoral level reveals that there is significant sectoral variability in labour cost per person day. The coefficients of variation vary between 25 and 30, and in absolute terms the labour cost per person day in the highest paid sectors (industry group 30 in India) is almost twice that in the lowest paid sectors (Tables 3.8a and 3.8b).

Sri Lanka exhibits a pattern in wage growth somewhat different from that in India and Pakistan. Wages in almost all segments of industry, commerce, services and government employees declined between 1985 and 1993. The only exception was agriculture which saw a rise from a index value of 116.6 in 1985 to 136.6 in 1993. Agriculture in this case almost entirely refers to the plantation sector. The industry- agriculture differential in wages which was in favour of industry in the 1960s had almost disappeared by 1984 and subsequently has been in favour of agriculture. This has largely been due to the Government's adherence to the structural reform package in the mid 1970s. This has involved "reversion from earlier across the board state interventions to a bi-partite / tri-partite mechanism of bargaining [which] has meant longer time lags in adjusting to minimum wages. Periodic adjustment in living allowances gave a saw-toothed pattern to real wage behaviour compared with built in indexation which provides automatic adjustment. In a majority of the wage boards the built in indexation

---

25. Irfan and Ahmed (1985).
26. Maḥmood and Qasim (1994).
27. Naqvi and Kemal (1994).

arrangements have been terminated."[28] These adjustments have implied a rise in the quantum of industrial disputes and a reversal of the earlier trend of declining incidence of strikes and lockouts.

An assessment of whether these mechanisms for wage determination have increased or decreased labour market flexibility depends on a number of factors. First, at the aggregate level the evidence of a link between growth in wages relative to the growth in labour productivity is mixed. In India and Pakistan the growth in real wages has tended to be faster than the growth in labour productivity, though since 1991, the process of reforms has increased productivity relative to labour costs. In Sri Lanka, at aggregate level, the growth in labour cost would be comparable to aggregate change in labour productivity. However, for the non-agricultural sectors there may have been a squeeze on real wages, in part compensating for the earlier periods of higher growth in real wages.

In addition, the shift to non-wage compensation in both India and Pakistan is reflective of an attempt to impart greater flexibility to labour cost. Indian evidence suggests that non-wage payments have closer correlations with productivity and would increase the flexibility of adjusting labour costs to changes in demand.

The labour cost differential at the sectoral level reveals considerable variation in labour cost per person day. While the absolute level differences are indicators of the difference in skill requirements, the difference in the growth rates are a measure of the ability of a sector to adjust wage costs to differences in its growth pattern. A examination of the trends in real wage rates across key sectors (Table 3.4) reveals striking differences in the rate of growth varying from 0.2 per cent in cotton textiles to 3.3 per cent in sugar. A similar picture emerges if we examine the growth in terms of real labour cost per day.

Finally, we turn to the question of flexibility in wage costs across alternative occupations inside sectors and establishments. There is little evidence for this except as can be inferred from an examination of the occupational wage survey data for India (Table 3.9). Analyzing the range between maximum and minimum wages paid for different occupations we find that there have been dramatic changes in some industries, for example, in cashew cultivation the standardized range declines from 42 per cent to 12 per cent while in railway workshops it rises from 19 per cent to 30 per cent. However, attributing such changes in relative payments to internal flexibility is confounded by the fact that all the industries covered by the Occupational Wage Surveys (OWS) are not uniformly organized. For

---

28. Rodrigo (1994).

example, matches and cashew cultivation have large segments of unorganized workers. Further, even inside industries, different occupation groups are subject to different levels of organization. Thus it is possible that these changes do not reflect different rewards to skills but differences in wage bargaining power. To the extent, however, that employees in different occupational segments have not all seen uniform increases in wages, the wage structures are not completely rigid.

3.5 Minimum Wages And Labour Market Flexibility

Conventional economic analysis would suggest that the effect of minimum wages, when set above opportunity cost of labour, is to reduce labour market flexibility and raise the cost of employment. In discussions relating to minimum wages we come across two broad concepts. The first is a uniform minimum wage applicable to all workers and the second are minimum wages as applicable to different sectors and occupations. In general South Asian countries do not have minimum wages of the first type. Though in India some states have defined statutory minimum wages applicable primarily to categories of "sweated labour" quite widely. In the absence of a uniform minimum wage across all sectors we would expect that sector-specific minimum wages would raise minimum wages and lower employment in these sectors. In comparing South Asia to South East Asian countries it is seen that minimum wages are a higher proportion of average wage.[29] Anderson and another[30] suggest that in Bangladesh this may have taken place, as wages in covered industries were higher and employment of skilled and unskilled labour was reduced as compared to uncovered industries. This result is however subject to some caveats, as the authors note, that it is likely that establishments selected for minimum wages were not random but were in the first place more organized establishments with a higher component of skilled workers. This is particularly true when we note that selection of industries for the imposition of minimum wages are governed by considerations of political economy.

In India there are two forms of minimum wage, first is the already noted statutory minimum wage for scheduled employment and the other is the minimum wage set for particular classes of organized workers. If we examine the link between these different types of minimum wages, we find

---

29. Khan (1994); see also, Khan (1995).
30. See, Anderson, Hossain and Sahota (1991).

that in India[31] the minimum wages in most organized work places are higher than the statutory minimum; this was particularly true by the mid 1980s. A sharper contrast between statutory minimum wages and wages in organized sectors can be seen in the awards of the Pay Commissions and the Wage Boards. The Third Central Pay Commission drew explicit attention to the low ('normative') levels of statutory minimum wages fixed across the states relative to the wages of peons in the Central and State Governments and stressed the need to fix minimum wages for Central Government employees "in consonance with conditions prevailing in the country". The effective final award had minimum wages for Central Government Employees higher than the statutory minimum wages. Further, except in the case of the Central Wage Board for Leather and Leather Goods, the links between the Statutory Minimum Wages and the recommended minimum wages are tenuous. The minimum wages recommended by the Central Wage Boards and made effective in the late 1960s ranged from Rs.116 per month for the Sugar Industry in Central India to Rs.244 per month for Textile Workers in Bombay. As against this, the highest Statutory Minimum Wage in 1969 was Rs.125 per month in Punjab, and the lowest would be about Rs.46 per month in Madhya Pradesh in 1968. In later Pay Commissions the restraining influence seen in the case of the Third Pay Commission drops out of sight.

Secondly, the evidence from the South Asian countries indicates that the minimum wages for unskilled labour are close to if not less than 'normative' poverty line wages. Thus it is likely that at these levels on grounds of ensuring efficiency and productivity, the workforce in more organized industries would need to be paid higher than what may be deemed to be the social opportunity cost of labour. This will lead to higher minimum wages in the organized sectors.

The point, which emerges from this discussion is that the argument that minimum wages have reduced flexibility in wages is rather limited. What does get established is that observed "inflexibility" is limited to the organized sectors and is more likely a reflection of other impediments to flexibility in these sectors, as in weak collective bargaining mechanisms, than the effect of a wage floor restricting the domain of movement in wages.

3.6 Conclusion

Activist governments have followed social welfare policies in varying degrees that provide extensive legal protection for employment. In terms of

---

31. This is based on a comparison of the minimum wages paid as reported in the various occupational wage surveys. The results of this comparison are reported in Anant and Sundaram (1995); and ILO-SAAT (1996) Chapter 2.

complexity and extent of scope, with regard to various facets of legal protection, Indian labour legislation has possibly been by far the most comprehensive followed by that in Sri Lanka, Pakistan, Bangladesh and Nepal in that order.

The discussion in the above section highlights how concerns for labour welfare and employment security have created a legal framework that imposes a number of structural rigidities on employers in their attempts at adjusting labour requirements in the face of changes in technology and/or market demand. The most elaborate network of protection is probably in India where it is hedged by numerous constitutional guarantees, and the weakest framework is possibly in Nepal. The coverage of most of this formal protection is restricted to establishments larger than a specified limit and often to employees in regular jobs. However, in view of the fact that, except for Sri Lanka, the proportion of the workforce formally covered by legal protection and minimum labour standards is not more than 10 per cent in India and Pakistan and even smaller in the case of Bangladesh and Nepal.

The legal framework for dispute resolution has tended to involve the state as a key and often critical element to the process. In addition in India, and to limited extent in Bangladesh, weak systems for collective bargaining and the politicization of the dispute settlement mechanism have further weakened the link between labour costs and productivity.

The response of employers to these rigidities has been in three possible directions. One, so long as there is no escape from being in the legally protected segment wherever possible, employers tend to adopt the least labour-intensive technology. Two, instead of expanding employment in the existing unit they subcontract production to units in the informal or unorganized segment. Three, they set up new units in the small-scale unorganized segment to escape the higher labour costs that ensue from labour legislation. The net result of these three types of responses is the limited absorption of labour in the legal protected segment. This accentuated duality in the labour market in the economies of the region is further exacerbated by the quantity-quality trade-off in an overall environment of deficiency of reproducible tangible capital and unlimited labour supply. Within the formal sector itself, it is useful to make a distinction between public (or government) and private ownership. Privately owned units have found legal and extra legal ways of getting around the rigours of labour legislation whereas public sector units have been unable to do this for obvious reasons. The policy response of activist governments has been in two directions. One, the extension of publicly-owned units and two, 'creating' jobs or employment in the publicly owned units irrespective of considerations relating to the productive utilization and commercial viability of the unit. Although this trend has been illustrated with reference to only the Indian context, the situation in neighbouring countries is possibly not too different.

Traditionally, units supplying infrastructural services (transport-mainly railways, communications and power) have been in the public sector due to considerations of market failure, positive externalities and their natural monopoly characteristics. Further since the Second Five Year Plan (1956-61) the scope of the public sector was extended to directly productive activities in the basic and heavy industries in order to give a boost to long-term growth and simultaneously reduce concentration of private economic power. Over time, further extension has taken place beyond the basic and heavy industries to start new units in all kinds of commercial activities such as trading, finance, hotels, production of bread, scooters and so on, with a view to 'generating' formal sector employment with assured quality. The extension did not stop here. It also embraced taking over loss-making private sector (termed 'sick') units into the public sector instead of closing them down. The basic motivation has been to 'protect' existing formal sector employment. With the well-known soft-budget constraint enjoyed by public sector units (at any rate till July 1991 in India), widespread feather-bedding took place apart from various inefficiencies arising from the non-commercial environment of public sector operation. Over time, therefore, public sector employment has become dominant within the formal or organized sector employment. Simultaneously the cost and scarcity of inefficiently produced non-tradable infrastructural services in the public sector have also been increasing with their negative spill-over consequences across the board which have further restricted the overall labour absorption in the formal sector. Reproducible tangible capital, too, had been invested in inefficient commercial activities in the public sector. While it 'generated' direct employment, its weak commercial viability has made sustaining that employment difficult in the absence of continued budgetary support. The continuation of this situation thus became conditional on remaining within tolerable fiscal bounds. The rising fiscal deficits in India in the 1980s were indicative of long-term unsustainability of public sector employment.

Two other policy measures to improve the qualitative aspects of employment deserve mention. They relate to legislation on minimum wages and trade unions. Here, the two can reinforce each other in the sense that, wherever trade-unions are well-organized, they can ensure enforcement of minimum wage legislation at least in the formal segment of the labour market. However, enforcement problems abound in the informal segment both because the trade union movement is weak and because enforcement costs are prohibitive for highly dispersed and decentralized informal sector activities. Thus, we find that minimum wages in certain occupations are lower than what may be termed as acceptable. In organized industries (or groups like public sector employees), wages are high. This further accentuates the difficulties of labour absorption in the organized sectors.

It would be overstating the case if we were to attribute the lack of flexibility in organized employment entirely to labour legislation. A good part of the explanation has also to lie with the rigidities in other dimensions of industrial and economic policies.[32] This detailed case study from India brings out the interplay of rigidities in banking, land and labour laws, and industrial licensing leading to industrial sickness.

---

32. Anant and Goswami (1995); and Anant et al. (1994).

4 Trade Liberalization, Economic Growth and Employment

4.1 Determinants of Trade Orientation

The process of globalization has been facilitated in modern times through easier and cheaper availability of transport and communication services resulting from advances in technology and efficiency and reduction in real costs. The extent of integration of different countries in this process has been shaped by the national policies relating to international trade in goods and services and in technology as well as by policies relating to factor movements especially capital. These policies govern the direction of trade which, in the sphere of merchandise trade can be conveniently conceptualized by the following index suggested by Bhagwati and Krueger (see Edwards, 1993).

$$B = \frac{E_m(1+t+r+PM)}{E_x(1+s+EP)}$$

where E_m and E_x are effective exchange rates applicable to imports and exports respectively;

t is the average tariff rate on imports;

r is the average *ad valorem* surcharge on imports;

PM is the rate of premium per unit of imports due to quantitative restrictions on imports;

s is the rate of export subsidies;

EP is the impact of export promotion measures per unit of exports;

This index can be interpreted as the ratio of profitability of selling in the domestic market to that of selling in the international market. In this framework, neutral trade regime is represented by $B = 1$ where the profits of selling in the domestic and international markets are equalized. Notice that free trade ($E_m = E_x$ and $t = r = PM = s = EP = 0$) is a special case of the neutral trade regime. The regime is said to shift to domestic market (or import-substitution or inward-orientation in the development literature) when B>1 and towards the international market (or export-orientation) when B<1. Three brief observations are necessary for the subsequent discussion. First, a neutral trade regime can exist in the presence of restrictions on transactions in international trade and hence can be distinct from free trade. Second, the components in the above equation for B stated within paranthesis in the numerator and the denominator bring trade and exchange rate-related government policies explicitly into the picture. Finally, while export promotion policies can directly affect exports, trade orientation can change towards exports with liberalization of restrictions on imports which reduce the numerator of B.

Policy-induced changes in trade orientation via their impact on relative profitabilities of selling in the domestic and international markets matched by corresponding responses from economic agents, bring about changes in comparative advantage. These, in turn, affect the employment of domestic primary factors, particularly labour, directly into the production of tradable goods and services in the economy and indirectly into the linked non-tradable activities. The post-Second World War experience of densely-populated low-income countries indicates that inward-oriented policies (B>1) have been associated with high capital-labour ratios and limited absorption of labour into the high productivity segment of the industrial sector. The excessive and prolonged concentration of policy on the limited size of the domestic market and the consequent insulation from international competition resulted in wasteful utilization of the scarce factor of production, namely, capital while limiting the absorption of the abundant factor of production, namely, labour. In contrast, the exposure to international competition associated with outward-oriented policies (B<1), especially in East and South-East Asian countries led to acceleration of exports, mostly resulting in rapid economic growth and rapid absorption of labour into fast-growing, high productivity, industrial activities which in turn facilitated a rise in real wages. The adjectives "excessive" and "prolonged" in the context of inward-oriented policies need emphasis while noting the contrast between the two sets of policies. This is because even the East and South-East Asian countries, that experienced export-oriented rapid growth, started with inward-oriented (B > 1) policies for initiating industrialization (with the sole exception of Hong Kong). However, they switched quickly to export-oriented policies either after realizing the growth-constraining limited size of the domestic market or after perceiving the boom in international markets or probably a combination of both.

In the final analysis, changes in the sectoral absorption of labour take place during the process of economic growth as a result of changes in the economic structure. Changes in the economic structure are brought about in response to (a) changes in the composition of domestic demand resulting from a rise in per capita real incomes, (b) changes in international trade possibilities, and (c) the supply-side changes in technological options. These responses to changes in (a), (b) and (c) require mobility of capital and labour across sectors from one use to another and from slow growing units to faster growing ones. This mobility is more often induced by better economic opportunities, but it is not uncommon to find it being forced on reluctant economic agents. The process of rapid economic growth involves equally fast and major structural changes requiring swift mobility of labour that leads to obsolescence, unemployment, dislocation and growing relative disparities in earnings along with faster generation of new employment opportunities (Kuznets, 1972). Consequently, "economic growth involves costs, conflicts and adjustments" (Abramovitz, 1989). Sustainability of rapid growth crucially depends on evolving socially acceptable conflict-resolution mechanisms and credible cost-sharing arrangements including social safety nets for alleviating immediate dislocation and unemployment. Many of these adjustments are governed by social customs, traditions, informal conventions and norms of behaviour. Historically, governments in the presently developed countries played an active role in providing safety nets in the short run, while facilitating, in the medium run, the evolution of credible conflict resolution mechanisms and socially acceptable cost-sharing arrangements along with improving access to skill acquisition and infrastructure for locational mobility. These aspects relating to society, polity and government constitute, what may be termed as, non-tradable, society-specific institutional software. Different societies exhibit differential social capabilities in developing this non-tradable institutional software. The post-Second World War experience shows that rapid growth has been generated by a mutually reinforcing interaction between such institutional software and the opportunities for international trade. The ability to develop appropriate institutional software governs the capacity of each society to use international trade as an instrument in the economic growth process (Kravis, 1970). The mainsprings of the growth process are recognized to lie in the incentive structure (Baumol, 1990) as it is reflected in the price signals emanating from the domestic and international markets, and responses of economic agents to these signals. These responses are, in turn, shaped by government policies, which are expected to provide an enabling environment and social and economic institutions that lay the rules governing the participation in economic activity and the associated rewards (North, 1990).

The trade orientation of the economy, as reflected in trade and exchange rate policies and society-specific institutional software together influence the degree of openness of the economy which determines the link between trade liberalization and employment. The degree of openness reflects the extent of integration of the given economy with the world economy, in terms of the trade in goods in services, exchange of technology and factor movements. There is no universally accepted quantifiable measure of the degree of openness because it is a complex multi-dimensional concept. A generally used, but crude, measure for this purpose is the trade ratio given by the ratio of the sum of the value of exports and imports to gross domestic products (GDP) at market prices. Trade liberalization tends to increase the trade ratio for a given country over time. Our interpretation for inter-country comparison is that the higher this ratio, the greater would be the pervasiveness of external economic transactions in national economic activity and hence the greater would be the degree of openness and the closer the link between trade liberalization and changes in the employment pattern in tradable goods and services in the economy.

4.2 The Asian Experience

Table 4.1 provides trade ratios (Column 5) for selected South and South-East Asian countries for 1994. It is apparent that the degree of openness is much higher in Sri Lanka (trade ratio of 83 per cent) than India with a trade ratio of 27 per cent, or Bangladesh with 31 per cent. We may, therefore, expect the aggregate employment impact of trade liberalization to be much higher in Sri Lanka than in India or Bangladesh. It is also interesting to note that China has a much higher trade ratio than India and as high a trade ratio as South Korea. Since the trade ratios in 1994 reveal the accumulated impact of using international trade as an instrument in the growth process, it follows that China, with the largest world population, has used it much more extensively than either India or Bangladesh. This gets reflected in their growth rates of GNP per capita during 1980-93 (column 4) along with a rise in the trade ratios. However, pointing towards the need for caution in drawing too strong a causal link between crude measures and GNP growth rates is the experience of Sri Lanka where GNP growth has remained low despite a high trade ratio of 83 per cent.

In contrast with countries of East and South-East Asia, South Asian countries have traditionally been much more inward-oriented, and experienced much slower growth during 1965-80 (Table 4.1, column 3). Halting and gradual trade liberalization started in most South Asian countries since the late 1970s following the two oil-price hikes of 1974 and 1979 and the resulting need for expanding exports in order to pay for the rising import bill of petroleum, oil and lubricants. Possibly in combination with other favourable factors such as agricultural growth, with the exception of Sri Lanka, other countries of South Asia, namely Bangladesh, India and Pakistan have experienced much faster growth during 1980-93 than during 1965-80. The question is how far does the export structure of these economies reflect their comparative advantage in labour abundant industrial products.

An ESCAP study[1] provides a picture of changing commodity composition of industrial exports in selected Asian and Pacific economies for 1965, 1970, 1975, 1980 and 1985-88. The categories of products are:

I.   Resource-intensive products (RI)
II.   Labour-intensive products (LI)
III. Differentiated goods (DG)
IV.   Scale-intensive products (SI)
V.   Science-based products (SC)

The rationale underlying this classification has not been explained in the ESCAP study. Our presumption is that technology sophistication would be greater and the value addition higher in the differentiated (non-homogeneous) and scale-intensive (homogeneous) products than in the resource-intensive and labour-intensive categories. The science based products would require high technology. The study covers five countries of South Asia (Bangladesh, India, Nepal, Pakistan and Sri Lanka.) In addition, four pioneers of export driven rapid growth viz., Japan, Republic of Korea, Hong Kong and Singapore, known as the Newly Industrializing Economies (NIEs), four countries of ASEAN, viz. Indonesia, Malaysia, Philippines and Thailand (referred hereafter as ASEAN-4), and China which has opened up since the late 1970s are covered in this study (see Appendix Table A-1 which is a reproduction of Table III.8 of the ESCAP study).

It is seen that the NIEs while being resource-scarce are labour-abundant whereas the ASEAN-4 have an abundant natural resource-base but lower density of population. Of the four NIEs, Japan had completed the first phase of labour-intensive industrialization by 1965 when SI products accounted for as high as 37 per cent of industrial exports, and labour-intensive (LI) and differentiated groups (DG) for 27-28 per cent each. By 1988, the Japanese economy experienced labour scarcity and the share of LI went

---

down to nearly 6 per cent, the share of science-based goods (SC) rose from 0.8 per cent in 1965 to nearly 12 per cent in 1988 and that of DG by 10 percentage points to 38 per cent. The Republic of Korea and Hong Kong started with much higher shares of LI products and graduated to product categories DG, SI and SC (Hong Kong only) over the period. Singapore exploited its locational advantage by importing primary natural materials and exporting natural resource-intensive industrial products which accounted for nearly half of their exports till 1975. Thereafter, they shifted to SI and SC products.

Of the ASEAN-4, Indonesia and Thailand have been gradually moving from RI to LI products while Malaysia and Philippines have progressed further to SI products. China has concentrated mostly on labour-intensive industrial products by using its abundant labour.

The pattern of changing comparative advantage seems to start with resource-intensive or labour-intensive products (depending on initial factor endowments). The progress after this is varied as some have moved to differentiated products, others to scale-intensive products and a few to science-based products.

Turning to South Asia, Sri Lanka started with a comparative advantage in resource-intensive products in 1965 and moved over to labour-intensive products by 1986. The remaining four densely populated economies of Bangladesh, Nepal, Pakistan and India focused on labour-intensive exports. Of these, only India has made a headway into differentiated, scale-intensive and science-based segments but the share of these segments remained small and fluctuating till the mid-1980s.

The Indian case deserves a comment as India had a headlong start in industrialization in the mid 1950s well before the NIEs (except Japan) and the ASEAN-4. Both India and China started with a heavy-industry-oriented strategy that focused on the domestic market, and whose size was limited at low levels of real per capita income and the resulting inward trade-orientation. For both the countries, this strategy went against their natural comparative advantage of abundant labour. While China opened up rapidly from the late 1970s, trade liberalization in India picked up only in the 1990s. In the intervening period, the NIEs embarked on labour-intensive industrialization oriented towards international markets and experienced much faster rates of growth (Table 4.1) and labour absorption in the industrial sector by progressing toward more advanced industrial exports. The ASEAN-4 and China too experienced faster growth and much higher rates of labour absorption in the industrial sector than India.

4.3 An Indian Case Study

In the light of the perspective provided by the Asian experience in the last section, we confine this section to an Indian case study partly because the data for other countries is not readily available an also because of the authors' familiarity with the Indian context. Even in the Indian case, inferences are based on piecing together data from different sources.

As mentioned earlier, a significant change in the trade orientation towards export markets has taken place since 1991. A halting and tentative process of deregulation was set in motion only in the late 1970s and gathered pace in the mid 1980s.

This section draws on diverse databases to examine the relationship between exports and employment. From the international trade data, changes in the composition of Indian industrial exports, according to the classification of the UN-ESCAP study, are investigated over the 15-year period from 1979 to 1994, during which policy changes have been taking place. Next, on the basis of the input-output tables for 1978-79, 1983-84 and 1989-90, the sectoral shares of exports in domestic gross output are analyzed to trace those sectors which depend mainly on export markets. Finally the case study draws on the two censuses of small scale industrial units for 1972 and 1987-88 to examine the impact on employment of two major export-oriented industries. Differences in levels of disaggregation as well as time periods covered in the three data sources severely constrain the empirical analysis. The information from diverse sources are combined with directional changes in policy to draw certain broad inferences regarding the connection between trade liberalization and employment.

Since the export composition of Indian industrial exports is given up to 1985 in the UN-ESCAP study, it excludes the period of faster growth in dollar value of Indian exports in the second half of the 1980s and wide-ranging trade liberalization in the 1990s. Using the Standard International Trade Classification (SITC) details of various broad 3-digit export categories given in the footnote of Table III.28 of the UN-ESCAP study (Appendix Table A-1), the time-series of the composition of Indian industrial exports are worked out from 1979 to 1994, the latest year for which *the UN Statistical Year Book of International Trade* is available. Unfortunately, the composition of industrial exports for the common years 1980 and 1985 in our re-calculation did not match exactly with the corresponding figures in the UN-ESCAP study. Presumably, the SITC classification has undergone some changes between the time the UN-ESCAP study was completed and our re-calculations.

We have not been able to trace the sources of differences. Our re-calculations appear in Table 4.2.

It is apparent (from Col. 8 of Table 4.2) that Indian industrial exports increased from US$ 3 billion in 1979 to nearly US$ 4.5 billion by 1986. In the second half of the 1980s they more than doubled to US$ 9.5 billion by 1990 and further to US$ 14.7 billion by 1994. The share of industrial exports in total exports fluctuated between 35 and 45 per cent during 1979 and 1986 and between 48 and 55 per cent during 1987 and 1994. Labour-intensive exports as a proportion of industrial exports fluctuated between 50 and 58 per cent during the period. Since this percentage applied to industrial exports that doubled in the second half of the 1980s and by another 50 per cent by 1994, clearly the corresponding direct employment expansion must have taken place in proportion to the volume of exports. A clear-cut upward trend ia also observed in scale-intensive exports whose share in industrial exports increased continuously from about 8 per cent in 1986 to a little over 20 per cent by 1994. While this is clearly a change in the direction of desirable diversification in the composition of exports, one may expect a lower direct employment elasticity in scale- intensive exports than in labour-intensive exports.

Having examined the changes in the composition of exports according to the broad categories in Table 4.2, the scanning of Indian exports at the 3-digit disaggregation level according to SITC was undertaken. Here the measure of revealed comparative advantage (RCA) suggested by Balassa is used. It denotes the share of Indian exports of product 'i' in the world exports of product i, and s_i denotes the share of aggregate industrial exports of India in the corresponding world industrial exports; the RCA is given by the ratio s_i to s_t . If RCA exceeds unity, India is taken to possess revealed comparative advantage in product i. It is clearly the net effect of interaction between the price of a product in the international market and the response of Indian suppliers. If India is a price taker in product i, and if price remains reasonably stable (which would be the case so long as the world technology frontier remains stable) then rising s_i would reflect increasing penetration in the world market in terms of volume. In this case, if RCA remains well above unity and rises in a consistent fashion, it is a reflection of Indian firms gaining competitive advantage in the world markets. Even where India is a significant supplier of commodity i, s_i would reveal price-quantity interaction and rising RCA with magnitudes remaining well above unity which would still indicate a gain in competitive advantage. A decline in RCA over time even while remaining above unity would be indicative of loss of competitive advantage due to the entry of other competitor(s) with cost and/or locational advantage.

Table 4.3 reproduced from the *Economic Survey, 1996-97* of the Ministry of Finance, Government of India shows that in SITC product categories, tea and mate (SITC 074), spices (SITC 075) and pearls, precious and semi-precious stones (SITC 667), India's share in the world market crossed the double digit mark lying between 10 and 16 per cent. In all other products, India could be taken to be a price taker so that a rising RCA while exceeding unity may be taken to reflect gain in competitive advantage.

For India, we traced the movements in RCA from 1980 to 1993 at 3-digit SITC level. Among the 2-digit SITC groups, two labour-intensive products recorded consistently high RCAs exceeding unity, viz. textile yarn, fabrics and made-up articles (SITC 65) and articles of apparel and clothing accessories (SITC 84). We note briefly the major trends among industrial products:

(a)   Consistently rising RCAs while remaining above unity were observed for the following products with broad RCA trends and years of maximum/minimum RCA in brackets.

SITC   651 : Textile yarn: 1.1 (1985) to 4.7 (1993)

653 : Woven man-made fabrics : 0.4 (1985) to 1.7 (1993)

667 : Pearls, precious and semi-precious stones: 8.2 (1980) to 19.0 (1993)

846 : Undergarments, knitted : 1.6 (1985) to 3.7 (1993)

848 : Headgear, non-textile clothing : 1.5 (1986) to 6.0 (1990)

851 : Footwear: 0.8 (1985) to 1.4 (1993)

(b)   Consistently falling RCAs while remaining above unity

SITC   652 : Cotton fabrics, woven : 13.8 (1980) to 7.0 (1993)

654 : Other woven textile fabrics : 16.1 (1980) to 3.0 (1993)

658 : Textile Articles NES : 18.0 (1980) to 7.0 (1993)

695 : Tools : 2.6 (1980) to 1.3 (1993)

697 : Base metal household equipment : 2.5 (1980) to 1.8 (1993)

843 : Women's outwear, non-knit : 12.0 (1981) to 5.3 (1993)

844 : Undergarments non-knit : 14.5 (1986) to 8.0 (1993)

(c)   Fluctuating RCAs:

659 : Floor coverings, etc.: 10.0 (1990) to 13.0 (1981, 1985, 1987)

845 : Outwear knit non-elastic : 1.6 (1992) to 3.0 (1981)

847 : Textile clothing accessories NES : 2.7 (1986) to 6.7 (1981)

We have reported the above 3-digit categories where India managed to retain RCA above unity in the range and period indicated against each category. In group (a), with the exceptions of 653 and 851, rising RCA is indicated for the remaining four products. In group (b), while declining competitive advantage is indicated, it is necessary to assess the extent of associated penetration. These are mostly new categories which started being exported in the early 1980s. In group (c), it is important to assess whether fluctuations originated in external demand or domestic supply. The 3-digit products listed above accounted for hardly 10 per cent of the total exports in 1994 or less than one-third of the industrial exports.

It may be noted that as late as 1994, India's trade ratio has been observed to be one of the lowest (see Table 4.1). Consequently, despite the crudeness of the trade ratio measure noted earlier, the impact of trade liberalization on national income originating in the tradeable sectors and indirectly on employment cannot be expected to be large.

The employment effects of trade liberalization can be indirectly assessed by observing changes in sectoral gross export ratio defined as the share of exports in sectoral gross domestic output. The expectation is that the higher the export ratio and the greater the share of sectoral exports in total manufacturing exports, the more extensive would be the employment effects. This, in turn, can be combined with an *a priori* labour intensity of the sector concerned to draw inferences about the employment impact.

Export ratios can be worked out from the input-output transaction matrix and in particular by combining the export vector in the final demand with gross output of the sectors. The Central Statistical Organization in India has so far provided three input-output transactions tables[2] on a comparable 115-sector basis for 1978-79, 1983-84 and a more recent one for 1989-90. No input-output transactions matrix has so far been worked out for the post-1991 reform period.

Table 4.4 presents six sectors for which export ratio exceeded 20 per cent in the latest available year 1989-90 and the share of sectoral exports in total manufacturing exports (US$ million) for 1989-90, 1983-84 and 1978-79. Table 4.5 presents the same information for ten more sectors for which export ratio in 1989-90 was between 10 and 20 per cent. With regard to Table 4.4, it may be noted that exports of gems and jewellery are included in other non-metallic mineral products (sector 71, line 6). This sector is import-intensive as it requires imports of precious stones and diamonds.

With the exception of tea and coffee processing (sector 31) which is resource-intensive all the remaining five sectors in Table 4.4 are known to

---

2. These transaction matrices are provided in terms of what is described in the terminology of input-output analysis as commodity X industry tables. The rows of these tables indicate the sectoral utilization pattern of each sector's total supplies (consisting of gross output plus imports) given according to commodity classification. Columns, on the other hand, reflect the input absorption pattern which is given according to the industry classification which includes main and by-products produced in the sector.

be labour-intensive. Of these five, ready-made garments (sector 48) and gems and jewellery (sector 71) are new products whereas the remaining three have been the traditional exports. Exports expanded in all the five because of the relocation of these industries away from labour-scarce developed countries. Of these, ready-made garments is the most export-oriented industry with the highest export ratio of 70 per cent with gems and jewellery (sector 71, non-metallic mineral products), and leather and leather products (sector 55) comes next with export ratios between 50 and 55 per cent. The combined share of these three export-oriented industries in manufacturing exports declined from 38 per cent in 1978-79 to 30.6 per cent in 1983-84 and further to 28.5 per cent in 1989-90. While the share of ready-made garments in total manufacturing exports was maintained, the reduction in the share of gems and jewellery was not made up by a rise in the share of leather and leather products between 1983-84 and 1989-90. However, with rising total dollar value of manufacturing exports, direct employment expansion in these industries might be attributed to their export-orientation and hence indirectly to trade liberalization. In the remaining three sectors, the share of the domestic market (given by the complement of the export ratio) was dominant and their share in total manufacturing exports is either very small or declining. The six sectors in Table 4.4 accounted for a little over 35 per cent of Indian manufacturing exports.

The ten sectors in Table 4.5, each with an export ratio of between 10 and 20 per cent, had a continued share in manufacturing exports of a little under 16 per cent in 1989-90. Of these ten sectors, miscellaneous food products (sector 38) was possibly labour-intensive. Jute, hemp and mesta products (sector 46) was natural-resource intensive whereas the remaining eight were mostly scale-intensive sectors where export shares increased between 1983-84 and 1989-90. It may also be recalled that share of scale-intensive products in industrial exports showed a sharp increase between 1979 and 1994 (Table 4.2). However, with the dominant share of the domestic market in these products (reflected in low export ratios), employment expansion attributable to export expansion may be expected to be moderate.

The 16 sectors (out of 115) included in Tables 4.4 and 4.5 together accounted for a little over half of manufacturing exports in 1989-90. By implication nearly half the manufacturing exports took place in 1989-90 from the remaining 99 sectors (see Appendix Table A-2 for export ratios and export shares) with very low export ratios.

What conclusions can be drawn from the foregoing analysis?

One, the predominantly export-oriented, labour-intensive industries in India have been confined mainly to one sector (ready-made garments) or at best to three sectors with leather and leather products and gems and jewellery comprising the other two sectors. Most exporting industries have been focusing on the domestic market as evidenced by very low export ratios. This can be attributed mainly to the domestic market orientation of Indian trade policies with fairly stringent import restrictions. Two, trade liberalization undertaken by India in the early 1990s has been less extensive than that undertaken by other competitor countries. Even the impact of deregulation in the 1980s, reflected in a rise in the export ratios and export shares in 1989-90, has been diffused throughout the industrial sector. Consequently, the employment impact, may also be expected to be diffused. Direct quantification of this effect is difficult for two reasons. One, the export structure that we examined here follows the SITC or input-output based *commodity* classification whereas the employment figures are available by *industry* classification where employment in a given industry includes that in the production of main product as well as by-products. Two, since most industries cater mainly to the domestic market the increase in aggregate employment, wherever it has occurred, may be expected to be the result, in the main, of an expansion in the domestic market with marginal contributions from exports. This gets reinforced by the diffused sectoral contribution to exports.

Despite the diffused character of the impact on employment of trade liberalization, the direct impact is reflected in the sectors where (a) sectoral gross export ratio is high, and (b) the share of sectoral exports is increasing in a situation of rising aggregate exports. With this end in view we present two export-oriented industry level case studies where the industries were exclusively reserved for production in the small-scale sector. We have two censuses of small-scale industrial units providing data on employment at the disaggregated level. This analysis is based on two diverse data sources, namely, (i) the 115 sector input-output table based gross export ratios and shares of the sector's exports in total manufacturing exports, and (ii) gross export ratios and shares of industry's exports in total exports from small-scale industries. The levels of disaggregation as well as time periods covered in (i) and (ii) are different. Hence, the inferences are necessarily subjective rather than based on comparable data.

From our analysis of 115 sector input-output tables for 1978-79, 1983-84 and 1989-90, we find two sectors where the export share in sectoral gross output is dominant. These are ready-made garments (Sector 48) and leather and leather products (Sector 55). These industries recorded export shares (as per cent of sectoral gross output) of 70 per cent and 52 per cent respectively in 1989-90. These industries have been exclusively reserved for production in the modern small scale units. Two censuses[3] of small-scale industrial units (CSSIU I and II, for short) with survey periods 1972 and 1987-88 have been conducted by the Development Commissioner, Small Scale Industries, Ministry of Industry, Government of India. We try to piece together information from these two censuses relating to the two industries with reference to export performance and employment expansion focusing on comparable characteristics. The first census (CSSIU-I) was carried out for the year 1972 when export growth was low, whereas the second census (CSSIU-II) for the year 1987-88 marks the period of significant export expansion.

Of the two sectors mentioned above, it may be recalled that exports of leather and leather products declined (in terms of share in value of total exports) from 7 per cent in 1978-79 to 5 per cent in 1989-90 whereas the garment exports maintained their share at around 11 per cent in both 1978-79 and 1989-90.

At the 2-digit industry level in 1972, exports of hosiery and garments (under which ready-made garments are included) accounted for about 9 per cent of total small-scale industry (SSI) exports amounting to Rs.1,504.0 million, whereas leather and leather products accounted for 31 per cent (CSSIU-I, Vol. 1, Table 6.1, p.47). In relation to total gross output, exports ratio was 56 per cent for hosiery and garments (CSSIU-I, Vol. I, p.73 for gross output) and 52.5 per cent for leather and leather products (CSSIU-I, p.20 for gross output). By 1987-88, the share in SSI exports of hosiery and garments increased to 29 per cent and that of leather products declined to 18 per cent. However, the export share in gross output declined in both to 33 per cent in hosiery and garments and 44 per cent in leather products (CSSIU-II, Table 11.1, p.119). It is possible, however, that the export share in ready-made garments might have increased, though information on exports is not available in CSSIU-II at the required level of disaggregation. Export share in gross output was as low as 17 per cent for the ready-made garments (SIC 2941) in 1972 (CSSIV-I, Vol. II, Table III, p.102).

Information regarding employment is available for ready-made garments (SIC 2641) and leather and leather products (SIC 29) from both the censuses. Total employment in all SSI units increased at the rate of 5.5 per cent per annum from 1.65 million in 1972 to 3.7 million in 1987-88. The employment in the two export-oriented industries rose faster at 8.7 per cent per annum from 21,981 in 1972 to 76,920 in 1987-88 for ready-made

---

3. Report on the Census of Small Scale Industrial Units, *January 1977 (referred to as CSSIU-I), and* Report on the Second All India Census of Small Scale Industrial Units, *August 1992 (referred to as CSSIU-II).*

garments and at 6.5 per cent per annum from 31,775 in 1992 to 81,663 in 1987-88 for leather and leather products.

A definitive inference regarding the relationship between exports and employment is difficult because of non-comparability between CSSIU and Input-Output Tables (covering large and small scale units) and because of the different years to which they pertain. However, if we take the rising share of garments in the value of total exports, it is possible to infer that the faster employment growth in SSI in ready-made garments can be largely attributed to exports. The same inference, however, is not possible in the case of leather and leather products where domestic market share in gross output is significant.

Some further indirect corroborative evidence is available in CSSIU-II which provides export share in gross output for certain major states in regard to hosiery and garments and leather and leather products (Table 11.4, pp.126-27). Seven states of Tamil Nadu, Uttar Pradesh, Delhi, Maharashtra, West Bengal, Gujarat and Karnataka together account for Rs.7037.2 million of hosiery and garment exports (or 97 per cent of aggregate hosiery and garment exports). Of this nearly 40 per cent is from Delhi with 69 per cent share in gross output. The second and the third highest exports of hosiery and garments took place from Tamil Nadu and Maharashtra accounting for 27 per cent and 17 per cent respectively of exports from the seven states. Export shares in gross output for both these states were nearly 33 per cent each. These three states are known to be major centres of garment exports from India. In comparison, the exports of leather and leather products are much less prominent both in terms of value of exports and export shares. We, therefore, conclude that direct employment expansion at an above average growth rate in ready-made garments has been induced by growth in the external markets.

Finally in Table 4.6, we present further evidence regarding the comparison between the exporting and non-exporting units in the garment industry located in Delhi and collected as part of CSSIU-II and analyzed in a recent paper by Bhavani and Tendulkar (1998). The table provides key ratios for exporting and non-exporting units categorized according to three forms of business organizations, namely, proprietorship, partnership and limited (liability) companies. The following findings emerge from a close examination of Table 4.5.

One, the scale of operation measured by gross output per unit goes up as we move from single proprietorships to partnerships to limited companies for both the exporting and non-exporting units.

Two, efficiency in a labour-intensive industry, measured by the share of wages and salaries in gross output, is greater (in the sense of a *lower* wage share) among the exporting units than among the non-exporting units within each form of business organization.

Three, exporting units are more homogeneous, in the sense of having similar magnitudes of share of wages and salaries in gross output, than non-exporting units across forms of organization.

Four, exporting units on the average provide *higher* employment per unit *and* pay a higher (skill-adjusted) wage rate while recording a *lower* wage share than non-exporting units. An explanation of this apparently paradoxical observation is straightforward. So long as higher wage rates are offset by higher productivity (reflected in the greater efficiency of exporting units) *both* the wage rate and employment can rise while maintaining viability of the unit. Greater efficiency is forced on the exporting units by having to operate in a price- and quality-sensitive internationally competitive market.

Five, the data relate to units in the garment and apparel industry which is exclusively reserved for production in the small scale units. Even within the segment of small scale units, larger scale units operate in the export markets while incurring a higher share of sales expenses. In other words, accessing competitive international markets requires not only a larger share of sales expenses but also a larger scale of operations, in order to maintain acceptable quality, reliability and timeliness of supply. This casts serious doubts about the desirability of a reservation policy for the export-oriented small scale industries.

To recapitulate, the Indian case study puts forward three propositions:

First, even though industrial exports, in dollar value terms, exhibited a reasonable growth since the mid 1980s, the share of labour-intensive exports remained fairly stable while the share of scale-intensive exports rose steadily. The direct effects on a per-unit basis of labour-intensive exports is expected to be larger (in proportion to the volume of exports) than that in the case of scale-intensive exports. For scale-intensive exports, sophisticated technology, *cetris paribus* would restrict labour absorption while value addition would raise it. It should be obvious that if the volume of growth is large enough then both the quality and quantity of employment would improve. The realization of these potential benefits requires much more aggressive participation in international trade than has been attempted by the South Asian countries.

Secondly, in order to generate a substantial direct employment effect, a significant proportion of gross output of exportable industries needs to be devoted to exports. Most industries in India direct their output predominantly to the limited size of the domestic market rather than to the export markets. The domestic market oriented trade and exchange rate policies followed over the years are responsible for this outcome. This is consistent with the lowest trade ratio for India even amongst the South Asian countries noted in Table 4.1. The other countries of South Asia are no different even though Bangladesh has emerged as a low labour cost competitor to India in textiles in recent years.

Thirdly, predominantly export-oriented labour-intensive industries with expanding external demand such as apparel and garment experienced faster than average employment growth. The data for garment exporting units located in Delhi shows that exporting units provide higher employment per unit and pay a higher (skill adjusted) wage rate than non-exporting units. They manage this through greater efficiency than non-exporting units. Greater efficiency, in turn, is attained by exporting units having to operate in quality and price sensitive external competitive markets. The non-exporting units, in contrast, operate in non-competitive, price- though not quality-sensitive domestic markets with a greater tolerance of inefficiency.

What are the implications of the foregoing propositions for productive labour absorption and labour market policies?

In our view, low rates of economic growth and capital-intensive industrialization resulting from inward-oriented import substitution policies have been mainly responsible for inadequate rates of productive labour absorption in the South Asian countries. A radical change in past policies towards much more aggressive participation in international trade is clearly indicated by the recent experience of rapid growth in China and other East and South-East Asian countries.

A rapid growth through export orientation requires an internationally competitive industrial structure and efficient (non-tradable) physical infrastructure. The Indian case study of export-oriented garment and apparel industry indicated that exporting units operating in a price- and quality-sensitive internationally competitive environment were able to combine higher employment per unit as well as higher (skill adjusted wages) through greater efficiency than non-exporting units. In other words, efficiency forced by competition reconciles the quality and quantity dimensions of employment.

Although rigidities in the formal segment of the labour market in South Asian countries have contributed to, rather than been the main cause of limited productive labour absorption, their continued presence is bound to affect adversely the transition to an internationally competitive industrial structure necessary for export-oriented growth.

The transition to flexible formal sector labour markets in South Asian countries is bound to involve involuntary labour displacement. This would require the evolution of cost- sharing and conflict-resolution mechanisms emphasized in Section 4.1 which are essential also for sustainable rapid growth.

5 Looking Ahead : Employment Policy Options for South Asia

This final chapter examines the employment policy options available to and the nature of trade-offs involved in the choice of alternative instruments of policy intervention faced by the economies of South Asia.

5.1 Labour Force Projections

Among the countries of South Asia, Sri Lanka is the most favorably placed in the matter of labour force expansion over the next 15-20 years with the prospects of lowest expansion - between 1 and 1.25 per cent per annum. Nepal and Pakistan are at the other end of the spectrum with expansion rates of between 2.7 per cent (Nepal) and 2.75 per cent (Pakistan). In terms of absolute additions, while a little over 0.3 million would be added annually to Nepal's labour force, in Pakistan this figure would be close to 1.25 million. The World Bank's population projections for Bangladesh (World Bank, 1995) suggest a significant slowdown in the rate of population growth from a level close to 2 per cent per annum during 1990-95 to about 1.7 per cent per annum over the two decades 1990 to 2010. Assuming that an increase in the rate of schooling in the younger age groups roughly compensates for a higher share of the population in the prime working age groups, the labour force would grow at the same rate as population and add about one million workers per year. A recent study on India by Pravin Visaria (1997) suggests that over the period 1997 to 2012 the net additions to labour force in India would be approximately 1.9 per cent per annum implying a net addition to the labour force of approximately 11 million per annum..

The above set of numbers relating to the projected expansion in the labour force in the economies of South Asia should be considered in the context of limited labour absorption in the past in the organized sectors with higher than average productivity. If productive employment is to be provided to the growing labour force at progressively higher real wages, the corresponding requirements of productivity growth and hence much higher overall rates of economic growth should be obvious. If overall rate of economic growth is low as has been the case, then the imperatives of labour absorption are bound to conflict with those of productivity growth. Elasticity of employment with respect to output is, after all, the obverse side of growth in labour productivity. And growth in labour productivity is a necessary condition for sustained improvement in the quality of employment.

5.2   Summary of Findings

In addressing policy issues in this context we start by recapitulating some of our principal findings. The past experience of sectoral labour absorption in the South Asian countries surveyed revealed one positive and several negative features. The positive feature relates to the rising levels (albeit at slow rates) of labour productivity and wage rates in both the (legally protected) organized and unorganized segments of the economy. The major negative feature is the low absolute levels of initial labour productivity which get reflected in low levels of real per capital income.[1] These features especially in the Indian subcontinent are associated with poor quality of labour in terms of high rates of illiteracy (much more so among women than men), high rates of underemployment, prevalence of gender discrimination, high rates of youth unemployment and the prevalence of child labour.

With the exception of Sri Lanka, reported aggregate rates of open unemployment have not been very high. This is not surprising since, in the absence of the provision of social security by the state, very few people can afford to remain unemployed. In terms of the sectoral composition of the workforce, the share of agriculture and allied services has indeed declined in all the countries of the region. However, a much steeper decline has taken place in the share of this sector in real GDP so that productivity per worker relative to average productivity has declined sharply often accentuating the inter-sectoral inequality in productivity per worker. Equally importantly, the decline in the share of workforce in agriculture and allied services has been absorbed not in the organized segment with higher than average labour productivity but in the unorganized sectors with lower than average labour productivity. In other words, there has been an accentuation in the organized-unorganized duality in the countries of South Asia.

---

1. Notice that per capita income is the product of average per worker productivity multiplied by worker-population ratio (WPR). With limited WPR, the major source of low level per capita income is clearly low average per worker productivity.

What are the factors responsible for the negative labour market outcomes in the South Asian countries in the process of development? Two factors were investigated: labour legislation and labour policies in Chapter 3 and inward-oriented development strategy followed by most South Asian countries (with the possible exception of Sri Lanka since the late 1970s) in Chapter 4.

Labour legislation and labour policies impinge on the operation of the labour market. Two major facets of labour legislation were discussed; viz. (a) legal protection of income, job and employment; and (b) legislation relating to industrial dispute settlement. India has the most complex and comprehensive law with regard to protection and provisions of dispute resolution. The weakest framework is possibly in Nepal.

The dispute settlement mechanism, too, has the effect of discouraging healthy collective bargaining and tends to involve the state as a key and often critical actor in a time-consuming legal process. The undesirable result has been a weak system of collective bargaining and the unnecessary politicization of the dispute settlement mechanism. Because of considerations relating to costs of enforcement on the part of the government and unequal access to the legal system, the effective and sometime legally specified coverage of most of this legislation has been confined to larger establishments and to workers with regular jobs constituting the formal or organized segments of the labour market. The network of labour legislation strengthened often by favourable judicial verdicts and case law, has imposed constraints on the employer in adjusting the hired labour input in response to changes in technology and market demand. The proportion of the workforce covered by labour legislation is not more than 10 per cent of the total workforce in India and Pakistan and even smaller in Bangladesh and Nepal. The limited coverage may be the result of high enforcement costs and complex regulations. The employers in the formal organized segments may have devised mechanisms to ascertain a limited degree of flexibility. These mechanisms have consisted of increased reliance on contract labour, subletting out production to units in the unorganized sector and introducing non-wage related incentive payments in the total compensation to labour. While these mechanisms did result in some elements of labour-market flexibility, the cost of effective employment in the formal segment did go up. The labour legislation-induced constraints also discouraged the organized sector units from adopting labour-intensive technologies, even where they were available and in general induced them to minimize use of hired labour on a regular legal basis.

Compounding this process was the role played by the state in expanding the public sector. This expansion was initiated for various reasons ranging from market failure, externalities, natural monopolies arising out of conventional neoclassical economics to the agenda of economic socialism and even protecting formal sector jobs from the natural processes of 'creative destruction' resulting from competition and the product cycle. This has led the State to become a dominant and integral part of a complicated political economy which sustained the rigidities in the labour market. Minimum wage legislation formed the third and rather limited component of this activist employment policy.

5.3 Policy Options

Our analysis highlights the underlying trade-offs between the quality and quantity dimensions of productive employment. Further it is noteworthy that, even in legislation, quality of employment has been specified primarily in terms of three concepts of security of job, income and employment. Income security involves legally enforceable rights to receive contracted wages and salaries and other associated job related pecuniary benefits including bonus. Job security involves a secure relationship between the person and the job-description for which (s)he is hired within an organization. Employment security involves legal protection against arbitrary lay-offs/ retrenchment. These different types of measures have attracted differing levels of criticism with job and employment security being viewed as relatively larger impediments to flexibility. This also raises the possibility *of a trade-off among different dimensions of quality of employment* where a mechanism of collective bargaining preserves the quality of employment along with some (but not all) dimensions in order to impart flexibility along the quantity dimension in terms of the volume of labour absorption.

Turning to the informal or unorganized segment of the labour market, policy-initiatives have been motivated by apprehensions about technological unemployment in traditional occupations and the need for poverty alleviation. The unorganized segment is expected to attract increasing attention especially in the context of rising labour force growth rates and perceived limited possibilities of formal sector labour absorption.

Policy responses to prospects of technological unemployment have been two-fold: (a) protection of traditional craft-based occupation from competition with domestic as well as external large-scale units, and (b) promotion of these occupations by removing the handicaps they face in successfully competing with the large-scale mechanized units.

Protection from competition with the large scale units has taken the form of high tariffs on competing imports, high or graded excise duties on domestic large scale producers and reservation of certain categories of products for exclusive production in the traditional sector. Apart from difficulties of effective enforcement these measures have not succeeded in tackling two basic problems of the traditional occupations. The first one relates to the overcrowding or over-capacity relative to existing market size resulting from free entry of other small scale producers so that protection of large scale producers does not necessarily prevent unemployment or underemployment. The second problem is one of very low productivity of traditional craft-based occupations which limits their earning capability even in the presence of expanding markets.

Promotional measures seek to remove the handicaps faced by these occupations because of their limited access to credit, input-supply, upgraded technology and internal and external markets. Promotional measures are clearly superior to protective measures as the removal of handicaps enables this segment to compete successfully in the market place whereas the protective umbrella perpetuates dependency. However, promotional measures at present rely almost exclusively on the government machinery which is inadequately equipped to handle the widely dispersed and decentralized set of traditional activities.

The foregoing discussion with reference to the promotional and protective policies in the context of craft-based traditional occupations applies with equal force to geographically dispersed modern small scale units which lie nearer to the large scale factory segments in terms of technology than the traditional occupations.

In many dimensions, the issues relating to self-employment generation are the same as those discussed above in connection with technological unemployment. These are mainly micro-credit based activities which either create additional physical assets or technologically upgrade the existing skill cum physical asset-base. Mostly, these are activities complementary to agriculture. They aim at improving income-earning capability in a sustained fashion. The problems, of overcrowding and over capacity, too, are identical to those discussed in the context of technological unemployment.

Wage-employment generation programmes provide at best temporary income-supplements to earning members of the poor households. They range from disaster-relief programmes at one extreme to mainstream development programmes at the other. In disaster-relief programmes such as drought-relief public works, generation of purchasing power gets overwhelming priority over productivity of employment. In mainstream development programmes, on the other hand, the major objective is to promote long-term development and not employment creation. There exists a wide range between these two extremes in trying to combine productivity and employment creation in various degrees.

The adverse impact of rigidities in the formal segment of the labour market on organized sector labour absorption could have been partially offset in the presence of high rates of economic growth. However, the South Asian economies in comparison with their East and South-East Asian counterparts, experienced low rates of growth.

There cannot be any uni-causal explanation of low rates of growth. However, the persistent and prolonged inward-oriented growth strategy followed by the countries of the region could be a major factor. Section 4 pointed out that changes in trade orientation induced by trade and exchange rate policy (via their impact on relative profitabilities of selling the domestic *vis-a-vis* international markets) when matched by corresponding responses from economic agents, brought about changes in the sectoral pattern of comparative advantages. These, in turn, affect the employment of domestic primary factors, especially labour, directly in the case of the production of tradeable goods and services and indirectly in the case of the linked non-tradeable activities.

Changes in the pattern of comparative advantage of the rapidly growing economies of East and South-East Asia were brought out by studying the changes in their composition of exports. These changes have been accompanied by high rates of industrial growth as well as rapid absorption of labour in the industrial sector with higher than average productivity per worker. However, the effectiveness of export-oriented growth depended crucially on the existence of reasonably flexible markets in capital and especially in labour. This was because rapid growth required equally rapid changes in the patterns of sectoral absorption of labour. No doubt, these changes resulted in costs of temporary displacement, dislocation and unemployment. They also generated conflicts between employees engaged in slow growing and fast growing industries. For rapid growth, therefore, it is necessary to devise credible cost-sharing arrangements and socially acceptable conflict-resolution mechanisms. In other words, policy-induced changes in trade-orientation constitute a necessary but not a sufficient condition for rapid growth. Additionally these changes need to be accompanied by the corresponding social adjustments to generate and sustain rapid growth. Most South Asian countries, with the possible exception of Sri Lanka since the late 1970s have been following the domestic-market oriented (or import-substitution) policies that have resulted in capital-intensive industrialization, and consequently low rates of economic growth and resulting low rates of productive labour absorption.

Seen against the backdrop just outlined, the Indian case study suggested two propositions.' One, potential benefits from an export-oriented growth strategy require much more aggressive participation in international trade than has been attempted. Two, employment effects of such growth to be visible, require industries which cater predominantly to the external markets.

A case study of labour-intensive and export-oriented industry of textile garments and apparel showed that because of greater efficiency induced by having to operate in the internationally competitive price- and quality-sensitive market, the exporting units provided *both* higher employment per unit and paid a higher skill-adjusted wage rage. Thus a case for reconciliation of the quality and quantity dimensions of employment is called for.

It is necessary to emphasise that what is being suggested here is not a limited sectoral or enclave expansion of foreign trade. This has already been tried in the South Asian countries with the creation of Special Export Processing Zones and other direct export promotion policies with little success. Enclave or sectoral development even if successful does not bring about the rise in productivity associated with an internationally competitive industrial sector. In markets for tradeable goods this can be achieved by opening up to external competition. And equally importantly, in the non-tradeable segment, suitable reforms in domestic laws and institutions are vitally needed to enhance the climate for capacity creation and fresh investment. It is important to change the operating environment which has tended to depress rate of return and failed to encourage quality consciousness. This requires changes not just in labour market institutions but in the wider spectrum of organized sector institutions.

To sum up, the study emphasizes that rapid economic growth based on efficient labour utilization can be a powerful tool for successfully reconciling the quality and quantity dimensions of employment. However, attainment of rapid economic growth would require not only a radical change in government policies towards aggressive participation in the international division of labour but also major changes in the institutions to permit flexibility in the utilization of labour as well as capital but also to encourage capacity creation with cost and quality consciousness in the production of vitally needed non-tradeables. Equally important for sustained rapid growth is the evolution of credible cost-sharing arrangements and conflict-resolution mechanisms to meet the challenging task of establishing a strong link between trade policies and employment.

REFERENCES

Anant, T.C.A. and Omkar Goswami (1995). "Getting Everything Wrong: India's Policy Regarding Sick Firms" in D. Mookherjee (ed.), *Indian Industry,* New Delhi: Oxford University Press.

Anant, and Sundaram (1995). *Wage Policy in India: A Review*, Delhi: Delhi School of Economics.

Anant, TCA and S. Gangopadhyay and Omkar Goswami (1994). *Industrial Sickness in India: Institutional Responses and Issues in Restructuring*, Ministry of Industries, Government of India, New Delhi

Abramovitz, M. (1989). *Thinking About Growth and Other Essays on Economic Growth and Welfare*, Cambridge: Cambridge University Press.

Anderson, Kathryn, H. Najmul Hossain and Gian S. Sahota (1991). "The Effect of Labour Laws and Labour Practices on Employment and Industrialisation in Bangladesh", *Bangladesh Development Review*, March.

Baumol, W.J. (1990). "Entrepreneurship - Productive, Unproductive and Destructive", *Journal of Political Economy*, Vol.98, No.5, Part I (October), pp.898-921.

Bhavani. T. A. and S. D. Tendulkar (1998). "Determinants of Firm Level Export Performance: A Case Study of Indian Textile Garments and Apparel Industry", Working Paper No. 58, Centre for Development Economics, Delhi: Delhi School of Economics.

Burki, A.A. and U. Afaqi (1996). "Pakistan's Informal Sector: Review of Evidence and Policy Issues", *Pakistan Journal of Applied Economics*, Summer, Vol.XII, No.1.

Chaudhry, A.A. (n.d.). Economic Reforms, Industrial Restructuring and Labour Market Reforms in Pakistan" (mimeo).

Dreze Jean and Amartya Sen (1995). *India: Economic Development and Social Opportunity*, New Delhi: Oxford University Press.

Edwards, S. (1993). "Openness, Trade Liberalisation and Growth in Developing Countries", *Journal of Economic Literature*, Vol.XXXI (September), pp.1358-93.

ESCAP (1991). *Industrial Restructuring in Asia and the Pacific*, Bangkok.

ILO-SAAT (1995). *Sri Lanka: Employment Promotion and the Development of Micro and Small Enterprises*, New Delhi.

_____ (1996). *India: Economic Reforms And Labour Policy*, New Delhi.

_____ (1997a). *Employment in Nepal: Prospects and Policies – A Report for the Inter-Agency Task Force on Employment and Sustainable Livelihoods*, New Delhi.

_____ (1997b). *Pakistan: An Employment Strategy*, New Delhi.

Irfan, M. and Aziz Ahmed (1985). "Real Wages in Pakistan: Structure and Trends, 1970-84", *Pakistan Development Review*.

Islam, R. (1994). (ed.) *Social Dimensions of Economic Reforms in Asia*, New Delhi: ILO-SAAT.

Jacob, P. (1986). " A Note on Concept of Work and Estimates of Workforce: An Appraisal of the Treatment of Activity Relating to Non-Marketed Output", *Sarvekshna,* No: 27, Vol. IX, No. 4, April 1986.

Johri, C.K.(1997). "India" in *International Encyclopedia for Labour Laws and Industrial Relations*, Boston: Kluwer Law and Taxation Publishers.

Khan, Abdul Hamid (1997). "Pakistan" in *International Encyclopedia of Labour Law and Industrial Relations,* Boston: Kluwer Law and Taxation Publishers.

_____ (1995). "Structural Adjustment, Labour Market and Employment", *Asian Development Review*, Vol. 13, No.2.

Korale, R.B.M. (1997). *Unemployment and Wages: A Case Study of Sri Lanka*, Department of Census and Statistics, Government of Sri Lanka, Colombo.

Kravis, I.B. (1970). "Trade as Handmaiden of Growth - Similarities between the Nineteenth and Twentieth Centuries", *Economic Journal*, Vol.80, No.320 (December), pp.850-72.

Kuznets, S. (1972). "Innovations and Adjustments in Economic Growth", *Swedish Journal of Economics*, Vol.74, No.4 (December), pp.431-51.

Mahmood, Zafar and Mohammed Ali Qasim (1994). "Wages versus Fringe Benefits in the Large Scale Manufacturing Sector of Pakistan", *Pakistan Development Review,* 33:4.

Naqvi, Syed Nawab Haider (1994). "Stabilization, Structural Adjustment and the Labour Market: Issues and Evidence from Asia" in Islam (1994).

North, D. (1990). *Institutions, Institutional Change and Economic Performance,* Cambridge: Cambridge University Press.

Rehman, Masihur (1994). "Structural Adjustment, Employment and Social Protection for Workers in Bangladesh" in Islam (1994).

Rodrigo, Chandra (1994). "Structural Reform and the Labour Market in Sri Lanka" in Islam (1994).

Sundaram, K. (1989). " Female Workforce Participation Rates in Rural India: An Inter-state Analysis" in A.V. Jose (ed.), *Limited Options: Women Workers in Rural India,* New Delhi: ILO-ARTEP.

Tendulkar, Suresh D. and K. Sundaram (1995). "Social Exclusion Mechanisms, Processes and Labour Market Outcomes: An Indian Case Study", Delhi: Delhi School of Economics (mimeo.), September.

UNDP (1994). *Human Development Report, 1994,* New York: Oxford University Press.

UNDP (1997). *Human Development Report, 1997,* New York, Oxford University Press.

Venkatratnam, C. S. (1997). "Competitive Labour Policies and labour Laws in Indian States", LARGE Policy Paper # 24, New Delhi.

Visaria, P. (1990). "Concepts and Measurement of Unemployment and Underemployment in Asian Countries: A Comparative Study", Asian HRD Network Working Papers, New Delhi: ILO-ARTEP.

Visaria, P. (1997). "Youth Unemployment in India: Its Level, Nature and Policy Implications" (mimeo), New Delhi: Institute of Economic Growth.

World Bank (1995). "Bangladesh: Recent Economic Developments and Priority References", Washington: World Bank Country Report Number 13875-80.

Table 2.1 : Population and Labour Force in South Asia : Early 1980s - Early 1990s.

(million)

Country	Year	Population	Work Force	Labour Force
Bangladesh:	1984-85	97.80	29.00	29.50
	1990	109.00	50.10	51.20
India:	1983	718.11	302.32	308.23
	1993-94	895.09	374.39	381.94
Nepal:	1981	15.02	6.85	NA
	1991	19.53	9.19	NA
Pakistan:	1982-83	89.12	25.85	26.91
	1993-94	124.45	33.01	34.69
Sri Lanka:	1981	14.85	4.85	NA
	1996	17.77	5.28	6.08

Notes: a) Estimates of Workforce/Labour Force for 1990 in Bangladesh are based on a wider definition of WF/LF by which female LFPR rises from 10.6% to 63.4%.

b) Estimates for 1994 do not cover the Northern and Eastern Provinces of Sri Lanka. Population estimates (all ages) for 1994 (excluding Northern and Eastern provinces) are obtained by adjusting the Survey estimates of Population 10+ by the share of 10+ population in the total as reported in, Central Bank of Sri Lanka, *Annual Report*, 1996.

Sources: Bangladesh: World Bank (1995).
India: 1. Pravin Visaria (1997).
                    2. *Sarvekshana,* Journal of the NSSO, Government of India, New Delhi, March 1989.
                    3. National Sample Survey Organisation (NSSO) Report No. 409, *Employment-Unemployment in India, 1993-94,* Government of India, New Delhi, March 1997.
Nepal :   ILO-SAAT (1997a).
                    ILO-SAAT (1997b).
Sri Lanka: 1. Korale (1997).
                    2. *Quarterly Report of the Sri Lanka Labour Force Survey 4th Quarter, 1996,* Department of Census and Statistics, Government of Sri Lanka, August 1997.

Table 2.2 : Labour Force Characteristics of the Usual and Current Statuses in India and Sri Lanka

Panel A
Worker-Population Ratios and Unemployment Ratios

(per 1,000)

	Usual Status		Current Weekly		Current Daily	
	WPR	UE	WPR	UE	WPR	UE
India:						
1983	421	19	360	45	334	
1993-94	418	20	385	36	353	
Sri Lanka:						
1990	295	174	332	159	NA	NA
1994	306	129	322	131	NA	NA
1996	311	118	329	114	NA	NA

Note: WPR = Worker population ratio; UE = Unemployment rate.

Panel B
Share of Agriculture in the Work Force in India

(per 1,000)

Criteria	Usual	Current Weekly	Current Daily
1983	683	635	630
1993-94	639	612	602

Sources: India: *Sarvekshana,* April 1988 and March 1989; NSSO Report No.409, 1997, New Delhi.
Sri Lanka: Same as Table 2.1.

Table 2.3 Crude Worker - Population Ratios (%) by Gender in South Asia

	M	F	P
Bangladesh:			
1984-85	53.01	5.42	29.65
1989	52.69	39.58	46.35
1990	53.33	37.88	45.96
India:			
1983	53.84	29.50	42.10
1993-94	54.41	28.25	41.83
Nepal:			
1981	58.26	32.33	45.61
1991	49.28	44.84	47.06
Pakistan:			
1982-83	51.5	7.20	30.2
1994-95	44.19	6.63	25.95
Sri Lanka:			
1980-81	46.82	16.83	31.66
1994	44.99	19.49	32.24

Sources : As in Table 2.1

Table 2.4: Industrial Distribution of Work Force in South Asia: Early 1980s and Early 1990s

Country	Early 1980s				Early 1990s			
	A	M	I	S	A	M	I	S
Bangladesh	595	115	52	238	659	179	31	131
India	684	120	35	151	639	123	43	195
Nepal	912	6	2	80	812	27	13	148
Pakistan	529	136	66	269	500	101	66	333
Sri Lanka	473	131	57	339	395	151	71	393

Notes: 1. Periodization same as in Table 2.1
2. A: Agriculture and Allied Activities; M: Mining, Quarrying and Manufacturing; I: Infrastructure covering Electricity, Gas and Water, Transport, Communication and Storage, and Finance, Insurance, Real Estate and Business Services (in the case of Nepal, it also includes construction); S : Other Services.
3. For Bangladesh the estimates for 'Early 1990s' relates to 1989. The distribution for 1989 is strongly influenced by the sharp rise in the share of women in the total workforce from 9 per cent to 41 per cent following the use of a more inclusive definition of work in the 1989 Survey.

Source: As in Table 2.1

Table 2.5: Labour Productivity by Industry Groups in India, Pakistan and Sri Lanka in PPP Dollars : 1994

Country	Per capita GDP in PPP $1994	Male WPRs (per 1,000)	Productivity Per Worker (PPP Dollars)				
			Total	A	M	I	S
India	1348	504	2673	1294	4999	9767	3555
Pakistan	2154	442	4873	2715	9147	12864	5380
Sri Lanka	3277	450	7282	3998	10515	17535	7471

Notes: A: Agriculture and Allied Activities; B: Mining, Quarrying and Manufacturing; I: Infrastructure covering Electricity, Gas and Water Supply; Transport, Communications and Storage, and, Finance, Insurance and Business Services and Real Estate; S : Other Services. All worker participation rates are by reference to the Current Weekly Status. PPP refers to Purchasing Power Parity and WPR refers to Work Participation Rate.

Source: 1. Estimates of per capita GDP in PPP $ 1994 are taken from UNDP (1994).
2. Male WPRs: Table 2.3 [except for India]. For India, male WPRs on Current Weekly Status have been computed from NSSO Report 409.
3. Sectoral Shares in Work Force: As in Table 2.1.
4. Sectoral Shares in GDP: *National Accounts Statistics.*

Table 2.6: Industrial Distribution of Workforce (WF) and Gross Domestic Product (GDP) and Relative (RLP) and Absolute (ALP) Labour Productivity at Constant Prices : India, 1972-73 - 1993-94

	1972-73				1983				1993-94			
	Share in WF	Share in GDP	RLP	ALP (Rs.)	Share in WF	Share in GDP	RLP	ALP (Rs.)	Share in WF	Share in GDP	RLP	ALP (Rs.)
1.Agrl. & Allied Activities	73.78	45.63	0.618	2334	68.56	38.70	0.564	2531	63.85	31.01	0.486	2960
2.Mining+Quarrying	0.43	1.45	3.372	12734	0.60	1.81	3.017	13540	0.72	1.97	2.736	16666
3.Mfg.+Repair Services	8.96	17.79	1.985	7496	10.74	20.25	1.885	8460	10.73	21.40	1.994	12146
4.Electricity, Gas, Water	0.17	1.38	8.118	30658	0.28	1.91	6.821	35613	0.37	2.68	7.243	4412
5.Construction	1.87	5.30	2.834	10703	2.24	4.86	2.170	9739	3.25	4.61	1.418	8638
6.Trade, Hotel + Restaurant	5.14	11.31	2.200	8308	6.33	12.88	2.035	9133	7.61	13.61	1.788	10891
7.Transport, Storage, Communications	1.78	3.97	2.230	8422	2.49	4.95	1.988	8922	2.88	5.72	1.986	12097
8.Other Services	7.86	13.18	1.677	6333	8.76	14.63	1.670	7495	10.60	19.00	1.792	10915
9. Total	100.00	100.00	1.000	3777	100.00	100.00	1.000	4488	100.00	100.00	1.000	6091
3(a). Regd. Mfg.	2.27	10.16	4.476	16906	2.31	12.30	5.325	23899	2.07	13.64	6.589	40136
3(b). Unregd. Mfg	6.69	7.63	1.141	4310	8.43	7.95	0.943	4232	8.66	7.76	0.896	5458
WF million	233.16				301.24				374.50			
GDP (Rs. Million)	880530				1351980				2281230			
Relative mean deviation	0.5632				0.5971				0.6567			

Notes: 1. Sectoral shares in workforce have built up by aggregation across the four segments: rural males; rural females; urban males; and urban females with the estimates of workforce provided in Visaria (1997).

2. GDP estimates are at constant 1980-81 factor-cost prices. They exclude GDP originating in "ownership of dwellings". Sectoral shares in GDP have been worked out by reference to this adjusted estimate of GDP.

3. Relative mean deviation, given by $\sum_{i=1}^{n} \frac{(y_i - l_i)}{100}$, where y_i is the ith share of the sector of GDP and l_i is the sectoral share in WF, measuring the intersectoral inequality in product per worker.

Sources:
1. As in Table 2.1
2. Visaria (1997).
3. Central Statistical Organization, *National Accounts Statistics* (various issues), Government of India, New Delhi.

Table 2.7: Industrial Distribution of Workforce (WF) and Gross Domestic Product (GDP) and Relative (RLP) and Absolute (ALP) Labour Productivity at Constant Prices : Pakistan, 1984-85 - 1994-95

	1984-85				1990-91				1994-95			
	Share in WF	Share in GDP	RLP	ALP (Rs.)	Share in WF	Share in GDP	RLP	ALP (Rs.)	Share in WF	Share in GDP	RLP	ALP (Rs.)
1.Agrl. & Allied Activities	50.88	29.02	0.570	6435	47.49	27.16	0.572	8086	46.82	26.09	0.557	8552
2.Mining+Quarrying	0.17	0.44	2.588	29216	0.15	0.59	3.937	55657	0.12	0.52	4.333	66529
3.Manufacturing	13.76	17.49	1.271	14348	12.24	18.73	1.530	21630	10.39	19.24	1.852	28434
4.Electricity, Gas, Water	0.69	2.46	3.565	40245	0.83	3.66	4.410	62344	0.82	4.22	5.146	79012
5.Construction	5.64	4.33	0.768	8670	6.63	4.38	0.661	9345	7.21	4.16	0.577	8859
6.Trade, Hotels + Restaurants	11.61	17.07	1.470	16595	13.25	17.40	1.313	18562	14.51	17.08	1.177	18072
7.Transport, Storage, Communications	5.23	10.76	2.057	23221	5.24	10.13	1.933	27327	5.07	10.64	2.100	32243
8.Other Services	12.03	18.43	1.532	17295	14.17	17.95	1.267	17912	15.06	18.05	1.999	18409
9. Total	100.00	100.00	1.000	11289	100.00	100.00	1.000	14137	100.00	100.00	1.000	15354
WF (millions)	26.92				29.83				33.26			
GDP (Rs. millions)	303,902				421,700				510,670			
Relative mean deviation		0.4633				0.4516				0.4756		

Notes:
1. Sectoral shares in workforce have been adjusted by pro-rata distribution across sectors classified under "Activities not adequately defined" to the extent of 0.63 per cent in 1984-85; 0.60 per cent in 1990-91; and 0.07 per cent in 1994-95.

2. GDP estimates are at constant factor-cost prices. They exclude GDP originating in "ownership of dwellings". Sectoral shares in GDP have been worked out by reference to this adjusted GDP.

3. Relative mean deviation, given by $\sum_{i=1}^{n} \frac{(yi-li)}{100}$, where y_i is the share of the ith sector of GDP and l_i is the sectoral share in WF, which measures the intersectoral inequality in product per worker.

Source: As in Table 2.1

Table 2.8: Industrial Distribution of Workforce (WF) and Gross Domestic Production (GDP) and Relative (RLP) and Absolute (ALP) Labour Productivity at Constant Prices : Sri Lanka, 1990-96

	1990				*1996*			
	Share in WF (%)	*Share in GDP (%)*	*RLP*	*ALP (Rs.)*	*Share in WF (%)*	*Share in GDP (%)*	*RLP*	*ALP (Rs.)*
1.Agrl. & Allied Activities	40.30	23.91	0.495	12,312	38.72	18.86	0.487	14,981
2.Mining+Quarrying	1.65	3.11	1.885	46,884	1.69	2.59	1.533	47,157
3.Manufacturing	13.73	17.86	1.301	32,358	15.24	21.46	1.408	43,311
4.Electricity, Gas, Water	0.62	1.34	2.161	53,748	0.52	1.48	2.844	87,546
5.Construction	4.02	6.98	1.736	43,178	5.60	7.02	1.254	38,574
6.Trade, Hotels +Restaurants	9.91	21.11	2.130	52,977	12.32	22.18	1.800	55,370
7.Transport, Storage, Communication	4.23	11.48	2.714	67,503	5.08	11.87	2.336	71,858
8.Other Services	17.54	14.22	0.811	20,171	20.84	14.54	0.698	21,471
9. Total	100.00	100.00	1.000	24,872	100.00	100.00	1.000	30,761
Total WF (million)	5.047				5.535			
GDP(in Rs. million) at 1982 Prices		125,294				170,272		
Relative mean deviation			0.5543				0.5231	

Notes: 1. Sectoral shares of workforce have been adjusted by pro-rata distribution across sectors of the category, "Not Defined" to the extent of 3.2 per cent in 1990 and 3.6 per cent in 1996.

2. GDP figures are at constant 1982 factor cost price. They exclude GDP originating in "Ownership of Dwellings". Sectoral shares relate to this adjusted estimate of GDP.

3. Relative mean deviation, given by $\sum_{i=1}^{n} \frac{(y_i - l_i)}{100}$, where y_i is the share of the ith sector of GDP and l_i is the sectoral share in WF, which measures the intersectoral inequality in product per worker.

Source : As in Table 2.1

Table 2.9: Educational Attainment by Gender, of the Employed Population in India, Pakistan and Sri Lanka 1994

(per 1,000)

Country/Sex	Illiterate	Literate upto Primary	Middle School	Secondary & above but below graduate	Graduate and above
India:					
Males	372	282	146	96	103
Females	743	150	49	27	37
Persons	492	240	115	73	80
Pakistan:					
Males	535	193	95	141	37
Females	808	71	15	70	36
Persons	568	178	85	132	37
Sri Lanka:					
Males	43	212	496	177	72
Females	130	215	358	172	126
Persons	69	213	454	175	88

Note: 1. Estimates for India relate to usual status work force aged 15 years and above. For Pakistan and Sri Lanka, estimates relate to currently employed population aged 10 years and above.

Source: As in Table 2.1.

Table 2.10: Prevalence of Underemployment among Currently Employed Persons in South Asia

Country/year	Prevalence of Underemployment (%)			Segments/ Sectors of High Underemployment
	Rural	Urban	Total	
Bangladesh:				
1983-84	NA	NA	17.10	NA
1989	NA	NA	18.70	NA
India:				
1983	11.66	6.44	10.64	NA
1993-94	17.73	9.44	15.84	NA
Nepal:				
1984-85	46.40	33.60	NA	NA
1995-96	47.50	38.10	47.00	NA
Pakistan:				
1982-83	15.50	7.20	13.40	Agriculture
1987-89	13.20	4.90	10.70	Agriculture
1993-94	13.30	6.30	11.60	Agriculture
Sri Lanka:				
1996	NA	NA	33.90	Agriculture; Mining and Quarrying; Construction

Notes: Underemployed are defined as those working less than 40 hours a week (or in the case of India 5 days in a week) in Bangladesh, India, Nepal and Sri Lanka; and, less than 35 hours a week in Pakistan. It excludes those who had a job but did not work at all during the reference week.

Source: As in Table 2.1.

Table 2.11: Alternative Measures of Underemployment by Gender and Rural-Urban Location: India, 1993-94

Description of Measures	Prevalence Rate (Per 1,000)			
	Rural Males	Rural Females	Urban Males	Urban Females
1.Proportion of Usual Status (PS+SS) Workforce Unemployed in the Daily Status	40	30	27	24
2.Proportion of Weekly Status Workforce Unemployed in the Daily Status	26	21	15	17
3.Proportion of Usual Principal Status Workers who did not work more or less regularly and:				
-Sought/ available for work on most days	69	89	37	49
-Sought/ available for work on some days	31	49	13	24
-Not sought available for work	20	36	11	23
-Total	120	174	61	96
4.Proportion of Usual Principal Status Workers (15 yrs+) who sought or were available for:				
-additional work	69	60	44	51
-alternate work	55	43	42	42

Source : NSSO Report No.409, 1997, New Delhi.

Table 2.12: Share of the Informal (Unorganised) Segment in the Work Force by Industry Groups in India and Urban Pakistan(%)

Sector	India			Urban Pakistan	
	1972-73	1987-88	1993-94	1972-73	1985-86
Agrl. & Allied Activities	99.3	99.3	99.4	100.0	100.0
Mining+Quarrying	21.8	54.7	59.0	NA	NA
Manufacturing Incldg Repair Services	72.8	81.1	82.1	34.6	71.1
Electricity, Gas and water	Nil	Nil	Nil	NA	NA
Construction	73.0	90.0	89.9	79.3	86.5
Trade,Hotel & Restaurants	73.2	80.2	82.6	98.9	98.8
Transport,Storage & Communication	36.5	62.8	71.1	61.5	68.0
Resident services	61.1	58.0	66.1	NA	36.3
Total	90.5	90.1	91.1	69.1	72.7

Sources : 1. Tendulkar and Sundaram (1995), for India.
2. Burki and Afaqi (1996), for Pakistan.

Table 2.13 : Status Distribution of Work Force in India, Nepal and Sri Lanka

(per 1,000)

	India		Sri Lanka		Nepal		Bangla-desh	Pakistan	
	1983	1993-94	1990	1996	1981	1991	1990-91	1982-83	1994-95
Employee Total	424	455	552	611	91	214	115	275	324
Regular/ Salaried	135	137	NA	NA	NA	NA	NA	NA	NA
Casual	289	318	NA	NA	NA	NA	NA		
Public	NA	NA	215	150	NA	NA			
Private	NA	NA	337	461	NA	NA			
Employer	NA	NA	18	24	NA	NA	*	*	*
Own-Act. Worker	365	545	292	268			263	409	411
Unpaid Family Worker	208		138	99			462	277	202
Not classified							160	39	63
All	1000	1000	1000	1000	1000	1000	1000	1000	1000

Note: * Data on employer and own account worker are presented together.
Source: Same asTable2.1.

Table 2.14: Unemployment Rates in South Asia by Gender and Rural-Urban Location

Country/ year	R_m	R_f	R_p	U_m	U_f	U_p	M	F	P
Bangladesh:									
1984-85	1.3	4.5	1.6	2.7	Nil	2.4	1.5	3.7	1.7
1987	1.1	1.0	1.1	2.4	6.7	3.5	1.3	1.4	1.4
India:									
1983 CWS	3.7	4.3	3.9	6.7	7.5	6.8	4.4	4.8	4.5
1993-94 CWS	3.0	3.0	3.0	5.2	8.4	5.8	3.5	3.8	3.6
1983 CDS	7.5	9.0	7.9	9.2	11.0	9.6	8.0	9.3	8.3
1993-94 CDS	5.6	5.6	5.6	6.7	10.5	7.4	5.9	6.3	6.0
Nepal:									
1984-85	NA	NA	2.7	NA	NA	8.2	NA	NA	3.1
1995-96	NA	NA	4.6	NA	NA	8.4	NA	NA	4.9
Pakistan:									
1986-87	2.8	1.0	2.5	4.7	2.0	4.5	3.9	1.1	3.1
1994-95	NA	NA		NA	NA		3.9	14.9	5.4
Sri Lanka:									
1990	12.1	22.8	15.9	14.4	27.5	18.4	12.5	23.5	16.3
1996	8.2	17.7	11.3	8.7	18.3	11.6	8.3	17.8	11.4

Notes: R_m : rural males; R_f : rural females; R_p: rural persons;
U_m : urban males; U_f: urban females; U_p : urban persons
M : males (rural + urban) F: females(rural + urban); P: Persons (rural + urban)
CWS" Current weekly status
CDS: Current daily status
n.a.: not available
Source: Same as Table 2.1.

Table 2.15 : Profile of the Currently Unemployed in Pakistan and Sri Lanka

Panel A

Percentage Distribution by Duration of Unemployment by Gender

Duration of Unemployment	Pakistan (1987-88)	Sri Lanka (1996)		
	Persons	Males	Females	Persons
Less than 6 months	59.6 (27.8)	17.0	11.7	14.4
Of which less than 1 month	22.7 (7.7)	NA	NA	NA
More than 6 months	40.4 (28.0)	83.0	88.3	85.6
Of which more than 12 months	NA	67.7	80.0	74.0

(Figures within brackets indicate the proportion of unemployed who are new entrants to the labour force and are in the specified category of duration of unemployment.)

Panel B
Percentage Distribution of the Unemployed by Level of Education

Level of Education	Pakistan (1993-94)			Sri Lanka (1996)		
	Males	Females	Persons	Males	Females	Persons
Illiterate/No schooling	39.8	75.9	51.2	0.6	1.6	1.2
Pre-matric/ grades 0-9	31.3	8.5	24.1	65.0	43.5	54.0
of which grade 5-9	NA	NA	NA	57.1	37.9	47.3
Matric and above	28.9	15.6	24.7	34.4	54.9	44.8

Source: As in Table 2.1

Table 2.16 Extent and Characteristics of Persons (15-59 years) who were Unemployed on All Seven Days of the Reference Week by Gender and Location: India, 1993-94

(Per 1,000 Persons)

Item	Rural Males	Rural Female	Urban Males	Urban Females
Proportion of Persons				
UE on all 7 days	27	10	43	18
Characteristic of Persons				
UE on all 7 days				
a) Share of Youth (15-24 yrs)	541	441	620	618
b) Head of Household	286	83	140	35
c) Duration of Current Space of Unemployment Greater than 6 months	489	349	678	787
d) Below secondary level of education	600	497	462	321
e) Sought full-time regular/ salaried work	516	359	727	786
f) Sought full-time casual labour	309	478	90	62
g) Sought work in non-Agrl. Activities	688	435	968	948
h) New Entrants to the labour force	549	419	721	803
Note: UE: Unemployed				

Source: NSSO Report No.418. 1997, New Delhi.

2.17 : Children in the Labour Force in South Asia

Bangladesh : Unemployed per 1,000 Persons in Labour Force among Children (10-14 yrs) : 1984-85

(per 1,000)

Item	Rural Males	Rural Females	Urban Males	Urban Females	Males	Females
Unemployment Rate	30	59	81	NIL	33	48

India: Work Force Participation Rates among Children (5-14 yrs): 1993-94

(per 1,000)

	WPR		Unemp. rate	Share in total Work force
Age Category	5-9	10-14	10-14	5-14
Rural Males	11	138	7	33
Rural Females	14	141	NIL	51
Urban Males	5	66	40	16
Urban Females	5	45	17	37
Total persons	11	117	7	35

Nepal: Work Force Participation Rates among Children (10-14 years): 1981 and 1996

(per 1,000)

	Males		Females		Persons	
Item	1981	1996	1981	1996	1981	1996
WFPR	613	NA	519	NA	569	356

Pakistan: Labour Force Participation Rates and Share in Work Force: 1982-83 and 1994-95

(per 1,000)

	Males		Females		Total	
Item	1982-83	1994-95	1982-83	1994-95	1982-83	1994-95
LFPR	330	166	83	57	215	116
Share in WF	76	44	141	97	84	51

Sri Lanka: Work Force Participation Rates among Children (10-14 years): 1996

(per 1,000)

	Males	Females	Persons
WPR	19	10	14
Share in WPR Force	4	4	4

Source: As in Table 2.1

Table 2.18: Per 1,000 Children (5-14 years) in the Work Force by Status of School Attendance, Type of Activity and Reason for Working by Gender and Location : India 1993-94

Item	Rural boys	Rural girls	Urban boys	Urban girls
School Attendance Status				
Attending school	203	104	171	222
Dropped out	783	883	829	741
Never Attended	14	13	NIL	37
All	1000	1000	1000	1000
Types of Activity				
Worked in Household Enterprise				
Agriculture	535	498	111	112
Non-Agriculture	118	135	308	296
Hired Worker:				
Agriculture	178	194	31	79
Non-Agriculture	169	174	550	513
All	1000	1000	1000	1000
Supplement Household Income	600	570	629	627
Labour Shortage in household enterprise	203	176	65	77
Acquire Skill	28	26	99	11
Meet Personal Expenses	13	14	34	12
Pass Time	22	22	18	11
Repay Loan	1	1	NIL	NIL
Others	132	191	154	262
All reasons	1000	1000	1000	1000

Source: NSSO, Report No. 409.

Table 2.19 : Labour Force Characteristics of Youth in South Asia

Bangladesh: Labour Force Participation and Unemployment Rates: 1989

(per 1,000)

Age Category	LFPR		Unemployment Rate		
	15-19	20-24	15-19	20-24	All Ages
Rural Males	744	657	22	25	11
Rural Females	615	714	29	13	10
Urban Males	524	681	64	44	24
Urban Females	254	294	65	33	67
Total Males	707	824	27	29	13
Total Females	552	649	31	17	14

India : Participation and Unemployment Rates and Employment Status of Youth (15-24) Work Force in Rural and Urban Areas 1993-94

(per 1,000)

Item	Rural Areas			Urban Areas		
	Usual	Weekly	Daily	Usual	Weekly	Daily
LFPR	582	531	496	391	381	367
Unemp. rate	36	62	94	136	158	182
Share in Total Unemployment	701	484	389	662	596	536
Share in Youth Work Force						
i) Self-Employed	567			441		
ii) Regular Salaried/ Wage employee	50			296		
iii)Casual labour	382			263		

Nepal: Work Force Participation Rates Among Youth (15-19) : 1981-1996

(per 1,000)

		Males	Females	Persons
LFPR				
	1981	692	513	607
	1991	496	493	494
	1996	NA	NA	612

Pakistan: Labour Force Participation Rates : 1982-83 - 1994-95

(per 1.000)

Age-group	1982-83	1987-88	1994-95
15-19	403	364	323
20-24	508	483	479

Sri Lanka :   LFPR and Share of Youth in Population, Unemployment and Labour Force : 1996

(per 1.000)

Item	15-19	20-24	15-24
LFPR	272	685	457
Unemployment Rate	368	292	317
Share in Population	101	82	183
Share in Labour Force	74	52	126
Share in Unemployment	240	390	630

Source: As in Table 2.1

Table 2.20 : Women in the Labour Force in South Asia in the Early 1990s

	Bangladesh	India	Nepal	Pakistan	Sri Lanka
No. of Women Workers (million)	19.70	121.63	4.39	4.0	1.60
No. of Women Unemployed	0.40	2.08	NA	0.7	0.40
WFPR (per 1,000)	379	283	448	66	195
LFPR (per 1000)	387	288	NA	78	244
Unemployment/ Labour Force Ratio (per 1,000)	20	17	NA	149	200
Sectoral Shares (per 1,000)					
Agr. & Allied Activities	715	761	905	NA	446
Mining, Quarrying & Manufacturing	216	104	13	NA	223
Infrastructure	-	7	2	NA	
Other Services	55	122	80	NA	
					331
Extent of Underemployment Among the Employed(per 1,000)	NA	333	504*	423	396**
Employment Status					
Employees	52	427	NA	NA	642
Employer			NA	NA	9
Own Account Workers	64	573	NA	NA	161
Unpaid Family Work	833		NA	NA	188

Note: * Estimates relate to 1984-85.

          ** Estimates relate to 1996 (Average over four quarters).

Sources: As in Table 2.1

Table 3. 2: Strikes and Lockouts

	Bangladesh	India	Pakistan	Sri Lanka
1986	46	1892	26	84
1987	18	1799	26	68
1988	9	1745	18	64
1989	12	1786	42	52
1990	5	1825	99	116
1991	3	1810	94	130
1992	11	1714	40	103
1993	11	1393	-	49
1994	2	1062	25	223

Table 3.3: Strikes and Lockouts: Workers Affected ('000)

	Bangladesh	India	Pakistan	Sri Lanka
1986	105.98	1644.9	12.93	36.68
1987	88.8	1769.88	12.99	22.65
1988	28.87	1191.03	8.23	20.21
1989	59.7	1364.25	29.66	42.84
1990	14.55	1307.86	61.58	65.94
1991	0.45	1342.02	116.31	63.76
1992	6.19	1253.22	73.36	50.31
1993	6.10	953.87	NA	7.88
1994	5.64	762.7	15.43	71.89

Source: ILO: *Labour Year Book* (various years).

Table 3.4: India: Growth in Real Wage Rates (1980-92)

Industry	Annual Rate of growth (%)
Cotton Textiles	0.2
Hydrogenated Oils	2.5
Sugar	3.3
Matches	2.4
Soap	1.3
Electrical Machinery	2.5
General Index	1.8

Source: *Indian Labour Journal*, Chandigarh: Labour Bureau.

Table 3.5: Labour Cost (LC) - Private vs. Public Sectors: All Industries(Rs./Personday in current prices)

Year	Public Sector		Private Sector	
	LC/day	of which wages (%)	LC/day	of which wages (%)
1984	56.14	81.90	51.79	78.5
1985	66.00	79.80	55.26	77.2
1986	71.58	80.40	60.74	76.6
1987	81.16	80.00	71.60	76.9
1989	107.13	80.40	88.19	76.6

Source: Labour Statistics under the ASI: Labour Bureau.

Table 3. 6: RealWage Rates: Organized Sector

	Bangladesh[1]	India[2]	Pakistan[3]	SriLanka[4]
1980	150	118	81	105.4
1981	138	115	81	96.2
1982	138	123	83	92.6
1983	144	120	95	82.5
1984	148	125	100	79.3
1985	172	132	104	86.9
1986	179	133	113	88.6
1987	324	134	123	93.9
1988	303	133	132	87.4
1989	286	138		96.6
1990		137		89.9
1991			138	97.0
1992				97.1
1993				89.8
Growth rate	7.1%	1.5%	4.8%	-1.2%

Source: 1. Bangladesh: ILO-SAAT: *Wage Rates for Production Workers* 1973/74 = 100.
2. Labour Bureau: *Index of Wage Rates*, general index, 1971 =100
3. ILO-SAAT (1997b); Real wages in large Scale manufacturing., 1984 = 100
4. Central Bank of Sri Lanka, *Wage Index for Industry and Commerce*, 1978 = 100

Table 3.7 Wages in the Informal Sector

	India[1]	Pakistan[2]	Sri Lanka[3]
1980	1.65		115.9
1981			98.3
1982			104.2
1983	1.71		100.4
1984		100	108.8
1985		102	116.6
1986		107	113.8
1987	2.36	110	110.8
1988		110	121.6
1989		108	125.7
1990	2.57	111	122.7
1991	2.44	110	122.2
1992		116	126.1
1993		105	136.6
Growth rate	3.6%	0.9%	1.9%

Source: 1. Dreze and Sen (1995): The numbers are real wages for male agricultural labour in Rs/Day at 1960 prices, Ministry of Agriculture data.
2. ILO-SAAT (1997b); Real wages for Rural Casual Workers, 1984 = 100.
3. Central Bank of Sri Lanka: Wage Index for Agriculture, 1978 = 100. The index refers to the plantation sector only.

Table 3. 8a India : Real Labour Cost Per Personday: Selected Industries ASI

Industry Groups

Year	0	20	23	30	31	33	35-36	Variation
1980	31.36	19.93	29.70	45.34	41.31	39.50	42.28	26.51
1981	32.77	21.88	30.56	47.85	36.07	39.19	42.96	25.37
1982	34.08	27.41	30.04	50.25	36.23	38.97	46.91	23.60
1983	35.82	24.67	32.95	54.00	42.05	39.42	50.56	26.84
1984	38.57	26.84	35.40	58.31	45.39	44.23	53.90	26.36
1985	39.30	26.65	36.98	59.26	43.13	39.66	54.10	27.36
1986	41.39	26.95	41.00	62.10	48.63	40.31	57.23	27.69
1987	42.68	28.24	40.66	62.70	49.60	40.97	60.29	27.83
1988	45.46	31.10	42.66	67.31	55.04	40.96	62.68	28.00
1989	46.20	32.17	41.49	73.31	60.90	42.08	65.64	30.88
1990	47.75	31.76	42.85	81.81	60.13	43.04	67.42	34.11
1991	43.78	31.96	41.83	76.60	60.07	38.28	64.57	33.40
1992	48.24	33.08	41.77	81.13	60.19	45.79	65.70	32.38
1993	47.65	33.54	41.92	78.05	60.46	48.32	68.63	30.58

Source: *Annual Survey of Industries*: Summary Results for Factory Sector.

Notes: Industry Groups are as per National Industry Classification: 1987.

1. The nominal magnitudes are deflated by the two digit GDP deflator, of the corresponding sector, calculated from National Accounts data.

2. Labour cost is gross payments to labour and includes emoluments to employees and expenditures on provident and other funds as well as staff welfare expenses.

Table 3. 8b Pakistan: Labour Cost Per Employee : Selected Industries ASI

Rs '000

Year	0	20	23	30	31	33	35-36	Variation
1980	12.44	13.96	9.30	20.48	14.50	14.33	14.71	24.45
1981	14.23	17.19	10.24	26.21	19.40	8.24	16.36	39.87
1982	17.06	19.21	11.59	28.30	18.42	24.85	17.33	29.52
1983	19.25	20.62	12.45	31.57	24.87	28.41	21.85	28.73
1984	21.08	23.52	13.98	34.93	24.17	27.18	23.72	27.48
1985	23.91	26.30	16.02	35.77	29.00	32.37	26.58	24.41
1986	27.05	27.72	17.96	42.31	29.56	41.98	30.74	29.18
1987	30.86	31.58	21.15	50.00	35.00	44.38	33.41	28.23
1990	42.68	39.54	29.98	77.67	48.24	72.86	48.82	35.44

Source: *Economic Survey of Pakistan* (various years).

Notes: The numbers are in nominal magnitudes.

1. Industry codes are as per the Indian National Indian Classification (NIC-87). Industry groups in the Pakistan Census of Manufacturing Industry are mapped on to the corresponding NIC-87 two-digit code.

2. Variation is the coefficient of variation for the corresponding row or column.

Table 3.9 : India: Wage Spread

Industry	I OWS 1958-59 (%)	II OWS 1963-65 (%)	III OWS 1974-75 (%)	IV OWS 1985-90 (%)
		Average spread:		
Cotton Textiles	6.86	17.02	7.73	10.50
Tea Factories			14.65	21.76
Aeroplanes, etc.	17.63	16.36	32.89	27.42
Bicycles	20.65	22.39	14.63	20.31
Elec. Machinery	17.63	25.21	22.07	
Motor Vehicles	14.51	25.50	24.08	9.04
Railway Workshops	19.91	28.17	26.29	30.55
Rough Casting	16.36	28.40	18.79	18.77
Cashew	42.08	32.03	22.82	12.20
Fine Chemicals	16.67	27.49	22.33	
Heavy Chemicals	16.67	17.22	19.80	
Hydro Oils	12.41	23.26	19.04	16.76
Matches	45.34	23.76	24.67	24.52
Petro Refinery	10.67	38.69	35.65	28.10
Soap	17.31	19.36	36.02	14.74
Sugar	8.51	20.87	9.97	14.72
Khandsari			5.27	2.90
Tyres			26.68	23.63
Iron & Steel			20.48	17.86

Source: *Occupational Wage Surveys* (various years).
Notes: The average spread is calculated by taking the difference between the maximum and minimum wage in each industry and expressing it as a percentage of the average of these two numbers.
OWS = Occupational wage systems.

Table 4.1 Annual Growth Rate of GNP per capita (1980-93) and Trade Ratio (1994) for Selected Countries

Country	Annual Growth Rate of GNP per capita (%)		Trade Ratio (%)
	1965-80	1980-93	1994
(1)	(2)	(3)	(4)
Bangladesh	-0.3	2.1	31
India	1.5	3.0	27
Nepal	N.A.	2.0	58
Pakistan	1.8	3.1	41
Sri Lanka	2.8	2.7	83
Indonesia	5.2	4.2	56
Korea, Republic of	7.3	8.2	63
Malaysia	4.7	3.5	192
Singapore	8.3	6.1	292
Thailand	4.4	6.4	99
China	4.1	8.2	63

Source: UNDP (1997), Table 26, pp.202-203 for cols (3) and (4); Table 25 pp.201-02 for column (5).

Table 4.2: Percentage Composition of Industrial Exports from India

S.No.	Year	Resource Intensive	Labour Intensive	Differentiated Goods	Scale Intensive	Science Based	Total Industrial Exports ($b)	Share of (8) in Total Indian Exports (%)
(1)	(2)	(3)	(4)	(5)	(6)	(7)	(8)	(9)
1.	1979	21.20	54.46	8.69	12.26	3.39	3.1038	42.27
2.	1980	14.54	57.61	10.02	11.98	5.85	3.3371	44.32
3.	1981	12.54	58.42	11.26	10.67	7.11	3.4464	43.74
4.	1982	15.04	54.01	11.28	11.45	8.22	3.1631	36.96
5.	1983	20.52	54.50	9.68	8.89	6.41	3.2804	34.69
6.	1984	20.54	55.16	9.02	8.46	6.82	3.9032	39.59
7.	1985	25.99	52.52	8.53	7.50	5.46	3.9529	43.98
8.	1986	20.93	52.74	13.13	7.86	5.34	4.4905	45.92
9.	1987	20.50	56.02	9.14	9.21	5.13	6.1152	50.59
10.	1988	17.98	52.14	10.47	12.23	7.18	6.6325	47.81
11.	1989	18.49	51.02	8.25	13.37	8.87	8.8448	51.89
12.	1990	16.00	54.12	7.72	13.71	8.45	9.5274	53.09
13.	1991	14.79	50.74	7.88	17.54	9.05	8.9091	49.77
14.	1992	13.10	57.57	5.99	17.94	5.31	11.5490	55.76
15.	1993	11.38	56.04	4.75	21.42	6.41	11.7072	52.64
16.	1994	11.10	56.65	5.76	20.18	6.31	14.7281	55.94

Notes: 1. Classification of industrial exports into categories mentioned in the column headings of (3) to (7) is the same as adopted by ESCAP Report, Table III-28 reproduced as Table A.1 of this study.

Source : *Statistical Year Book of International Trade (various years).*

Table 4.3 India's Share in World Exports by Commodity Divisions and Groups

Div. Sl. No.	Code Group	Commodity Division/Group	1970			1975		
			World (US $ million)	India	India's share (%)	World (US $ million)	India	India's share (%)
1	2	3	4	5	6	7	8	9
01		Meat and meat preparations	3584	4	0.1	7378	9	0.1
03		Fish, crustaceans and molluscs & preparations	-	-	-	-	-	-
04		Cereals and cereal preparations	6775	9	0.1	25133	16	0.1
	042	Rice	925	6	0.6	1984	12	0.6
05		Vegetables and fruits	1471	17	1.2	10104	154	1.5
06		Sugar, sugar preparations and honey	2700	26	1.0	11663	554	4.8
07		Coffee, tea, cocoa, spices and manufactures	5437	280	5.1	9133	438	4.8
	071	Coffee and coffee substitutes	3205	31	1.0	4580	73	1.6
	074	Tea and mate	587	196	33.4	933	292	31.3
	075	Spices	255	52	20.5	548	73	13.3
08		Feeding stuff for animals	-	-	-	-	-	-
12		Tobacco and tobacco manufactures	1713	43	2.5	3827	124	3.2
	121	Unmanufactured tobacco and refuse	1058	42	4.0	2357	119	5.0
	122	Manufactured tobacco	655	1	0.2	1470	5	0.4
22		Oilseeds and oleagineous fruit	-	-	-	-	-	-
28		Metalliferous ores and metal scrap	7357	193	2.6	13446	253	1.9
	281	Iron ore and concentrates	2373	158	6.7	4601	247	5.4
51		Organic chemicals	6648	9	0.1	20219	22	0.1
52		Inorganic chemicals	-	-	-	-	-	-
53		Dyeing, tanning and colouring materials	1615	8	0.5	3642	23	0.6
54		Medicinal and pharmaceutical products	2687	11	0.4	6503	29	0.4
55		Essential oils and perfume materials	916	10	1.1	3059	18	0.6
		toilets, polishing and cleaning preparations	-	-	-	-	-	-
57		Explosives and pyrotechnic products						
58		Artificial resins, plastic materials, cellulose esters & ethers	-	-	-	-	-	-
59		Chemical materials and products n.e.s.	-	-	-	-	-	-
61		Leather, leather manufactures & dressed fur/skins	1047	95	9.1	2380	200	8.4
	611	Leather	701	94	13.4	1540	189	12.3
	612	Manufactures of leather or of						

(Contd...)

(Contd...)

Div. Sl. No.	Code Group	Commodity Division/Group	1970			1975		
			World (US $ million)	India	India's share (%)	World (US $ million)	India	India's share (%)
1	2	3	4	5	6	7	8	9
		composition leather	132	1	0.6	355	4	1.0
	613	Fur/skins, tanned or dressed etc.	214	-	-	486	8	1.6
65		Textile yarn, fabrics, made-up articles	11371	461	4.1	23798	599	2.5
	652	Woven cotton fabrics	1436	98	6.8	3149	161	5.1
	653	Woven fabrics of man made fibres	3967	189	4.8	8038	191	2.4
	654	Woven fabrics other than of cotton or man-made fibres	270	2	0.8	547	5	0.9
66	667	Pearls, precious and semi-precious stones	2431	53	2.2	5707	128	2.2
67		Iron and steel	14540	132	0.9	40789	116	0.3
69		Manufactures of metals n.e.s.	4328	27	0.6	12053	74	0.6
71		Power-generating machinery & equipment	20884	25	0.1	54327	97	0,2
72		Machinery specialized for particular industries	10670	17	0.2	67016	102	0.2
73		Metal-working machinery	-	-	-	-	-	-
74		General industrial machinery & equipment & machine parts thereof	-	-	-	-	-	-
75		Office machinery and ADP equipment	-	-	-	-	-	-
76		Telecommunication and sound recording and reproducing apparatus and equipment	-	-	-	-	-	-
77		Electrical machinery, apparatus and appliances	-	-	-	-	-	-
78		Road vehicles (including air cushion vehicles)	-	-	-	-	-	-
79		Other transport equipment	-	-	-	-	-	-
84		Articles of apparel and clothing accessories	109	-	-	308	-	-
		Other exports	207521	605	0.3	555611	1398	0.3
		Total exports	313804	2026	0.6	876094	4355	0.5

Table 4.3: India's Share in World Exports by Commodity Divisions and Groups

Div. Sl. No.	Code Group	Commodity Division/Group	1980			1985		
			World (US $ million)	India	India's share (%)	World (US $ million)	India	India's share (%)
1	2	3	4	5	6	7	8	9
01		Meat and meat preparations	17832	67	0.4	15755	61	0.4
03		Fish, crustaceans and molluscs & preparations	12258	242	2.0	14335	337	2.4
04		Cereals and cereal preparations	41989	201	0.5	32643	211	0.6
	042	Rice	4355	160	3.7	2916	162	5.6
05		Vegetables and fruits	24018	259	1.1	23606	332	1.4
06		Sugar, sugar preparations and honey	16183	46	0.3	10113	0	0.0
07		Coffee, tea, cocoa, spices and manufactures	22121	879	4.0	20779	971	4.7
	071	Coffee and coffee substitutes	12979	271	2.1	11676	226	1.9
	074	Tea and mate	1631	452	27.7	1973	517	26.2
	075	Spices	1072	156	14.5	1188	229	19.3
08		Feeding stuff for animals	10322	164	1.6	8515	127	1.5
12		Tobacco and tobacco manufactures	3423	151	4.4	7822	140	1.8
	121	Unmanufactured tobacco and refuse	3423	151	4.4	3798	113	3.0
	122	Manufactured tobacco	-	-	-	4024	27	0.7
22		Oilseeds and oleagineous fruit	9487	30	0.3	7896	20	0.3
28		Metalliferous ores and metal scrap	30239	465	1.5	23137	557	2.4
	281	Iron ore and concentrates	6515	411	6.3	6154	478	7.8
51		Organic chemicals	31841	17	0.1	36923	25	0.1
52		Inorganic chemicals	15491	26	0.2	16318	22	0.1
53		Dyeing, tanning and colouring materials	7986	65	0.8	8024	62	0.8
54		Medicinal and pharmaceutical products	13918	109	0.8	15920	130	0.8
55		Essential oils and perfume materials toilet, polishing and cleaning preparations	7647	86	1.1	8136	56	0.7
57		Explosives and pyrotechnic products	630	1	0.1	840	0	0.1
58		Artificial resins, plastic materials, cellulose esters & ethers	27223	3	-	28456	5	0.0
59		Chemical materials and products n.e.s.	15960	8	-	16613	28	0.2

(Contd...)

(Contd...)

Div. SL No.	Code Group	Commodity Division/Group	1980			1985		
			World (US $ million)	India	India's share (%)	World (US $ million)	India	India's share (%)
1	2	3	4	5	6	7	8	9
61		Leather, leather manufactures & dressed fur/skins	5967	405	6.8	6444	534	8.3
	611	Leather	3415	342	10.0	4185	331	7.9
	612	Manufactures of leather or of composition leather	975	62	6.3	1233	202	16.4
	613	Fur/skins,tanned or dressed etc.	1577	1	0.1	1026	0	0.0
65		Textile yarn, fabrics, made-up articles	48884	1145	2.3	48218	1037	2.1
	652	Woven cotton fabrics	6632	351	5.3	6804	327	4.8
	653	Woven fabrics of man made fibres	9325	44	0.5	9735	20	0.2
	654	Woven fabrics other than of cotton or man-made fibres	3188	204	6.4	3462	167	4.8
66	667	Pearls, precious and semi-precious stones	18563	579	3.1	12073	1165	9.6
67		Iron and steel	68231	87	0.1	61891	46	0.1
69		Manufactures of metals n.e.s.	36840	221	0.6	32884	125	0,.4
71		Power-generating machinery & equipment	35722	88	0.2	38433	59	0.2
72		Machinery specialized for particular industries	58495	65	0.1	54707	97	0.2
73		Metal-working machinery	15671	32	0.2	12696	55	0.4
74		General industrial machinery & equipment & machine parts thereof	59443	67	0.1	53954	60	0.1
75		Office machinery and ADP equipment	24750	2	0.0	53604	30	0.1
76		Telecommunication and sound recording and reproducing apparatus and equipment	26799	11	0.0	47318	4	0.0
77		Electrical machinery, apparatus and appliances	60947	114	0.2	75739	121	0.2
78		Road vehicles (including air cushion vehicles)	127347	208	0.2	157446	126	0.1
79		Other transport equipment	41291	32	0.1	50709	27	0.1
84		Articles of apparel and clothing accessories	32365	590	1.8	38718	887	2.3
		Other exports	1027803	1912	0.2	890188	1293	0.1
		Total exports	1997686	8378	0.4	1930849	8750	0.5

Source: Economic Survey (different years).

Table 4.4 : Share in Total Manufacturing Exports for 1989-90, 1983-84 and 1978-79 of those Sectors whose Export Ratio Exceeded 20 % in 1989-90, India

S. No.	Sector No.	Sector Description	Export Ratio (%) in 1989-90	Share (%) in Manufacturing Exports in 1989-90	1983-84	1978-79
(1)	(2)	(3)	(4)	(5)	(6)	(7)
1.	37	Tea & coffee processing*	25.36 (2.44)	3.66	6.41	5.28
2.	44	Silk textiles	24.81 (15.98)	0.89	0.74	0.33
3.	48	Ready-made garments*	70.26 (12.47)	10.65	10.65	10.66
4.	54	Leather footwear	35.53 (14.41)	2.35	2.12	0.36
5.	55	Leather & leather products*	51.72 (17.35)	4.75	3.68	6.66
6.	71	Other non-metallic mineral products*	53.08 (8.54)	13.12	16.24	15.46
7.		Total (1 to 7)	- (10.28)	35.42	39.84	38.75
		Total Manufacturing Exports ($ million)	13875 (12.47)	6856		5389

Notes: Export ratio is defined value of exports as per cent of domestic gross output

1. *Registered export ratio exceeding 20 per cent in all the three years.

2. Miscellaneous manufacturing (sector 98) recorded export ratio of 24 per cent (1978-79) and 33 per cent (1983-84) which fell to 4 per cent in 1989-90.

3. Figures in bracket in column (5) indicate compound growth rate (percent per annum) in dollar value of exports of the sector between 1983-84 and 1989-90.

   Column (2) provides the sector number in the 115-sector input-output classification.

Source: Input-Output Transactions Matrices supplied by the Central Statistical Organisation

Table 4.5 : Share in Total Manufacturing Exports for 1989-90, 1983-84 and 1978-79 of those Exports whose Exports Ratio was between 10 and 20 per cent in 1989-90, India

S. No.	Sector No.	Sector Description	Ratio Export (%) in 1989-90	Share (%)in Manufacturing Export in		
				1989-90	1983-84	1978-79
(1)	(2)	(3)	(4)	(5)	(6)	(7)
1.	38	Misc. food products**	13.98	5.55 (32.04)	2.10	7.33
2.	46	Jute, hemp & mesta textiles	13.48	1.02 (0.78)	1.97	2.03
3.	60	Inorganic heavy chemicals	16.50	1.69 (56.81)	0.23	0.33
4.	61	Paints, varnishes, lacquers	11.33	1.43 (24.96)	0.76	0.70
5.	66	Soaps, cosmetics, glycerine	17.63	2.73 (18.75)	1.97	1.42
6.	79	Industrial Machniery (F & T)	13.38	1.18 (30.21)	0.49	0.57
7.	80	Industrial machinery (others)	12.08	1.00 (38.24)	0.29	0.21
8.	86	Batteries	10.79	3.22 (61.30)	0.37	0.23
9.	87	Electrical appliances*	10.07	1.24 (6.29)	1.74	1.40
10.	88	Communication Equipment**	15.16	1.49 (76.42)	0.10	1.39
11.		Total (1 to 10)	15.55	10.02 (21.01)	15.61	
12		Total Manufacturing Exports ($ million)	13875	6856 (12.47)	5389	

Source : Input-Output Transaction Matrices supplied by the Central Statistical Organization

Note: Export ratio is defined as the value of exports as per cent of value of gross output of the sector.

* Export ratio between 10 and 20 per cent in all the three years.

** Export ratio between 10 and 20 per cent in 1978-79 but not in 1983-84.

For unstarred sectors, export ratio fell below 10 per cent in 1983-84 and 1978-79.

Figures in brackets in column (5) indicate compound growth rate (per cent per annum) in dollars.

Value of exports of the sector between 1983-84 and 1989-90.

Column (2) provides the sector number in the 115-sector input-output classification.

Table 4.6: Mean Values for the Scale of Operation and Structural Ratios by the Form of Business Organisation and Exporting Category, India

Category	Units	Scale of Operation		Capital Intensity		Labour Productivity		WR	SE	Factor Shares		
		PRD÷U	L÷U	TK÷L	FK÷L	VA÷L	PRD÷L			SW	SM	SSE
(1)	(2)	(3)	(4)	(5)	(6)	(7)	(8)	(9)	(10)	(11)	(12)	(13)
Proprietorshiop :												
Exporting units	57	8653 (1.32)	31 (1.27)	45.85 (0.94)	39.61 (0.97)	116.37 (1.20)	291.48 (0.89)	11.29 (0.85)	54	0.08 (1.07)	0.59 (0.32)	0.25 (1.74)
Non-Exporting units	121	1199 (3.10)	12 (2.28)	20.92 (0.83)	17.96 (0.83)	17.77 (1.04)	61.11 (1.18)	6.18 (1.24)	46	0.25 (2.41)	0.53 (0.63)	0.07 (1.64)
Partnership:												
Exporting Units	66	17508 (1.31)	61 (0.95)	48.11 (0.98)	32.81 (0.99)	117.09 (1.53)	341.05 (1.27)	12.06 (0.85)	75	0.07 (1.33)	0.64 (0.26)	0.13 (0.84)
Non-Exporting Units	79	2546 (2.31)	18 (1.23)	22.74 (0.92)	18.95 (0.91)	28.998 (1.03)	109.301 (0.82)	6.42 (0.54)	25	0.13 (1.21)	0.65 (0.34)	0.08 (1.56)
Limited Companies:												
Exporting Units	64	22101 (1.66)	76 (1.04)	57.23 (080)	44.89 (0.72)	111.57 (1.80)	350.58 (1.57)	12.24 (0.67)	95	0.07 (1.11)	0.64 (0.23)	0.11 (0.75)
Non-Exporting Units	6	11256 (1.25)	46 (0.48)	45.03 (0.64)	39.89 (0.64)	65.42 (0.93)	219.09 (0.84)	10.27 (0.57)	5	0.07 (0.69)	0.66 (0.27)	0.13 (0.15)
All Units	395	8565 (2.26)	35 (1.48)	35.63 (1.09)	28.43 (1.00)	67.36 (1.93)	201.94 (1.63)	9.00 (9.29)		0.13 (2.55)	0.60 (0.40)	0.11 (1.80)

Source: Second Census of Small Scale Industrial Units, 1992.

Notes: PRD = Value of Production (Rs. 000), U = Number of Units, L= Number of Employees, TK = Total Capital (Rs. 000), FK = Fixed Capital (Rs. 000), VA = Value Added (Rs. 000), WR = Wage Rate per Person per Annum (Rs. 000), SE = Share of Employment of Exporting Group in the employment of the category of business form of organisation, SW = Share of Wages (ratio of wage bill to value of production), SM = Share of materials (Ratio of value of materials consumed to value of production), SSE = Share of Sales Expenses (Ratio of sales and other expenses to value of production).

Figures in parentheses are coefficients of variation.

Appendix 1

Table A.1 (Table III-28) Changing Sectoral Composition of Industrial Exports in Selected Asian and Pacific Economies (%)

Economics	1965	1970	1975	1980	1985	1986	1987	1988
RESOURCE-INTENSIVE								
Japan	5.9	4.3	3.6	3.5	2.3	2.1	2.2	2.1
Bangladesh	-	-	-	12.7	16.0	17.2	16.1	-
Sri Lanka	100.0	93.7	75.4	60.8	35.1	22.7	-	-
Hong Kong	0.6	0.7	0.6	0.9	0.9	0.8	0.9	1.2
India	10.8	15.0	25.4	14.5	25.2	-	-	-
Indonesia	-	97.4	98.9	85.2	74.7	68.5	70.9	65.1
Republic of Korea	21.0	17.4	11.1	6.8	5.3	4.4	4.3	-
Malaysia	89.0	90.4	80.1	57.9	45.8	32.0	30.3	29.0
Nepal	-	-	39.3	-	20.1	15.9	-	-
Pakistan	10.2	10.9	14.0	-	12.9	11.0	10.3	-
Philippines	94.9	86.7	74.9	51.9	44.1	39.5	-	36.2
Singapore	47.9	54.6	51.8	47.0	41.5	31.8	25.0	21.1
Thailand	92.4	89.3	47.3	38.3	16.7	11.2	9.9	-
China	-	-	-	-	20.2	11.7	11.0	-
Papua New Guinea	-	-	100.0	-	90.7	93.1	-	-
LABOUR-INTENSIVE[1]								
Japan	27.4	21.6	12.2	8.9	6.9	6.6	6.1	5.6
Bangladesh	-	-	-	84.3	81.6	79.6	81.5	-
Sri Lanka	0.0	6.3	12.5	35.3	60.9	72.1	-	-
Hong Kong	78.5	71.0	69.2	53.5	51.6	51.8	52.4	48.8
India	80.0	55.9	45.5	53.6	50.0	-	-	-
Indonesia	-	0.5	0.1	6.9	17.2	23.1	20.8	24.2

(Contd....)

---

1. Includes SITC Categories 65,691,692,695,696,697,699,84,851,821,898,899.

Table A.1 (Table III-28) Changing Sectoral Composition of Industrial Exports in Selected Asian and Pacific Economies (%)

Economics	1965	1970	1975	1980	1985	1986	1987	1988
Republic of Korea	59.9	68.8	56.5	46.0	37.5	41.2	39.7	..
Malaysia	1.9	2.2	5.5	8.8	8.5	10.3	11.1	11.6
Nepal	-	-	60.7	-	74.0	79.2	-	-
Pakistan	83.6	85.6	80.3	-	78.6	81.2	84.3	-
Philippines	5.1	6.4	19.9	31.5	29.6	30.7	-	31.3
Singapore	18.3	15.7	9.5	8.3	7.4	8.8	9.6	8.5
Thailand	7.6	8.8	39.5	35.1	47.1	49.2	52.3	-
China	-	-	-	-	56.9	62.6	61.5	-
Papua New Guinea	-	-	0.0	-	1.4	0.0	-	-
DIFFERENTIATED GOODS								
Japan	28.5	26.4	27.4	47.5	42.9	41.4	40.6	38.1
Bangladesh	-	-	-	1.2	1.4	0.8	0.4	-
Sri Lanka	0.0	0.0	5.3	2.3	2.7	3.5	-	-
Hong Kong	12.1	14.3	12.7	13.4	13.2	13.5	12.5	10.7
India	4.6	16.7	10.0	14.6	8.9	-	-	-
Indonesia	-	0.0	0.1	1.9	3.0	4.5	6.4	8.1
Republic of Korea	13.7	3.9	14.5	27.8	36.0	26.8	25.3	-
Malaysia	1.8	2.1	2.1	2.4	6.1	7.4	8.1	7.1
Nepal	-	-	0.0	-	5.9	4.9	-	-
Pakistan	2.2	1.7	3.7	-	4.5	4.6	3.3	-
Philippines	0.0	6.2	2.3	10.0	9.4	9.9	-	9.5
Singapore	9.3	6.1	5.2	9.5	7.7	9.2	9.3	9.6
Thailand	0.0	2.0	4.5	6.9	9.7	10.1	9.6	-
China	-	-	-	-	13.0	14.1	14.9	-
Papua New Guinea	-	-	0.0	-	1.7	0.5	-	-
SCALE-INTENSIVE[2]								
Japan	37.4	46.9	56.3	35.5	39.3	40.0	40.3	42.3
Bangladesh	-	-	-	1.7	1.1	2.5	1.6	-
Sri Lanka	0.0	0.0	3.3	0.5	0.9	1.3	-	-
Hong Kong	7.8	13.2	16.7	28.0	27.5	27.8	27.9	30.9
India	2.8	9.8	16.2	11.1	9.7	-	-	-
Indonesia	-	0.9	0.6	4.4	2.8	1.2	0.7	1.3
Republic of Korea	5.4	9.6	17.5	17.1	17.5	22.7	2.58	25.9

(Contd....)

---

2. Includes SITC Categories 51,52,53 533, 581, 621, 625, 629, 642, 663.9, 664, 665, 666, 67, 693, 694, 78, 79-792, 892, 893, 894.

Table A.1 (Table III-28) Changing Sectoral Composition of Industrial Exports in Selected Asian and Pacific Economies (%)

Economics	1965	1970	1975	1980	1985	1986	1987	1988
Malaysia	4.9	4.2	11.6	28.1	37.0	48.0	48.2	49.6
Nepal	-	-	0.0	-	0.0	0.0	-	-
Pakistan	2.5	0.8	1.2	-	1.2	0.6	0.1	-
Philippines	0.0	0.0	2.2	5.9	16.3	19.0	-	21.7
Singapore	21.6	21.5	31.1	30.8	30.9	35.1	37.8	40.2
Thailand	0.0	0.0	7.4	18.4	·22.9	26.6	24.1	-
China	-	-	-	-	5.3	7.2	8.4	-
Papua New Guinea	-	-	0.0	-	4.8	3.9	-	-
SCIENCE-BASED[3]								
Japan	0.8	0.8	0.6	4.7	8.6	9.8	10.9	11.9
Bangladesh	-	-	-	0.0	0.0	0.0	0.4	-
Sri Lanka	0.0	0.0	3.5	1.2	0.40.4	-	-	-
Hong Kong	1.0	0.8	0.8	4.2	6.7	6.1	6.4	8.4
India	1.8	2.7	2.9	6.3	6.2	-	-	-
Indonesia	..	1.2	0.4	1.5	2.3	2.7	1.3	1.2
Republic of Korea	0.0	0.2	0.3	2.3	3.7	5.0	4.8	-
Malaysia	2.5	1.1	0.7	2.7	2.7	2.3	2.3	2.8
Nepal	-	-	0.0	-	0.0	0.0	-	-
Pakistan	1.5	1.1	0.9	-	2.9	2.7	2.0	-
Philippines	0.0	0.8	0.7	0.7	0.7	1.0	-	1.2
Singapore	2.9	2.2	2.4	4.5	12.5	15.1	18.3	20.6
Thailand	0.0	0.0	1.3	1.3	3.6	3.0	4.0	-
China	-	-	-	-	4.7	4.5	4.2	-
Papua New Guinea	-	-	0.0	-	1.4	2.5	-	-

3. Includes SITC Categories 533,54,55,75,792,87.
Source: ESCAP (1991).

Table A.2 : Value of Exports as Per cent of Gross Output for Manufactured Commodities : 1989-90, 1983-84 and 1978-79, India

S.No.	2-digit Group	Input-Output Sector Number and Description	1989-90		1983-84		1978-79	
			Value of Exports (Rs. Million)	Exports as per cent of Gross Output	Value of Exports (Rs. Million)	Exports as per cent of Gross Output	Value of exports (Rs. Million)	Exports as per cent of Gross Output
(1)	(2)	(3)	(4)	(5)	(6)	(7)	(8)	(9)
1.	20-21	35 Hydrogenated oil (vanaspati)	-	0.00	0.0	0.0	0.0	0.0
2.		36 Edible oil other than vanaspati	4673.9	8.92	1483.9	2.81	1108.19	5.57
3.		37 Tea and coffee processing	8457.8	25.36	4530.6	23.95	2337.96	29.79
4.		38 Miscellaneous food products	12821.2	13.98	1485.0	3.20	3243.92	10.78
5.	22	39 Beverages	174.4	1.35	6.1	Neg	6.73	0.26
6.		40 Tobacco products	1273.3	3.39	199.3	0.01	906.51	7.89
7.	23	41 Khadi; cotton textile (handlooms)	950.0	4.19	925.1	4.43	534.87	7.27
8.		42 Cotton textiles	8704.0	5.42	2059.2	2.57	1699.29	3.27
9.	24	43 Woollen textiles	422.5	3.93	119.5	2.10	25.28	0.76
10.		44 Silk textiles	2059.7	24.81	524.8	6.17	147.34	5.95
11.		45 Art silk, synthetic fibre textiles	2299.0	2.29	318.1	0.69	404.58	2.53
12.	25	46 Jute, hemp, mesta textiles	2355.9	13.48	1394.1	15.80	896.66	16.24
13.		47 Carpet weaving	7772.0	6.54	2214.2	60.34	1175.56	63.31
14.		48 Readymade garments	24621.9	70.26	7527.1	36.38	4715.30	40.48
15.		49 Miscellaneous textile products	2634.4	4.91	548.1	3.28	947.64	11.97
16.	27	50 Furniture & fixtures-wooden	7.7	0.14	7.9	0.27	10.16	0.47
17.		51 Wood and wood products	457.9	2.00	319.9	1.60	123.70	1.24
18.	28	52 Paper, paper products, newsprint	1920.4	3.70	613.0	3.19	328.99	4.30
19.		53 Printing and publishing	557.5	1.50	350.3	2.12	224.16	2.95
20.	29	54 Leather footwear	5419.9	35.53	1496.2	19.15	159.52	3.98

(Contd...)

S.No.	2-digit Group	Input-Output Sector Number and Description	1989-90		1983-84		1978-79	
			Value of Exports (Rs. Million)	Exports as per cent of Gross Output	Value of Exports (Rs. Million)	Exports as per cent of Gross Output	Value of exports (Rs. Million)	Exports as per cent of Gross Output
(1)	(2)	(3)	(4)	(5)	(6)	(7)	(8)	(9)
21.		55 Leather & leather products	10981.9	51.72	2602.7	41.78	2947.69	73.47
22.	30	60 Inorganic Heavy chemicals	3911.7	16.50	161.3	1.65	147.19	2.22
23.		61 Organic Heavy chemicals	3655.3	9.20	268.1	2.64	163.67	6.15
24.		62 Fertilisers	3.8	Neg.	5.4	Neg	0.15	Neg
25.		63 Pesticides	913.0	7.65	41.6	0.86	15.64	0.98
26.		64 Paints, varnishes, lacquers	3309.6	11.33	539.7	5.23	309.43	5.74
27.		65 Drugs and medicines	5809.2	9.18	1282.2	5.81	443.93	4.50
28.		66 Soaps, cosmetics, glycerine	6305.0	17.63	1395.1	8.17	626.40	9.24
29.		67 Synthetic fibres, resin	1266.4	2.59	19.1	0.13	19.93	0.32
30.		68 Other chemicals	1146.4	1.99	798.0	3.42	116.56	1.16
31.	31	56 Rubber products	1746.8	3.55	376.2	1.73	209.72	2.48
32.		57 Plastic products	1076.7	2.88	237.8	2.62	79.26	2.97
33.		58 Petroleum products	5867.6	4.40	3403.1	4.28	243.51	1.16
34.		59 Coal tar products	0.6	Neg.	0.0	0.00	1.72	Neg
35.	32	69 Structural clay products	58.8	0.30	15.6	0.17	19.51	0.32
36.		70 Cement	114.9	0.28	7.6	Neg	13.96	0.35
37.	71	Other non-metallic mineral products	30333.8	53.08	11479.3	51.28	6838.72	38.08
38.	33	72 Iron & steel & ferro alloys	2006.0	2.74	28.2	Neg	637.86	5.32
39.		73 Iron & steel castings and forgings	1449.6	8.39	37.1	0.41	35.41	0.69
40.		74 Iron & steel foundries	1040.0	0.72	826.4	1.78	1786.46	7.39
41.		75 Non-ferrous basic metals	1558.2	1.79	210.0	1.47	997.36	11.51
42.	34	76 Handtools and hardware	1748.1	4.44	665.1	4.68	598.90	9.14
43.		77 Miscellaneous metal products	1959.7	1.70	787.2	3.43	649.41	7.35

(Contd...)

S.No.	2-digit Group	Input-Output Sector Number and Description	1989-90		1983-84		1978-79	
			Value of Exports (Rs. Million)	Exports as per cent of Gross Output	Value of Exports (Rs. Million)	Exports as per cent of Gross Output	Value of exports (Rs. Million)	Exports as per cent of Gross Output
(1)	(2)	(3)	(4)	(5)	(6)	(7)	(8)	(9)
44.	35	78 Tractors & agricultural implements	152.0	0.47	80.9	0.95	54.17	1.27
45.		79 Industrial machinery (F & T)	2716.7	13.38	343.4	4.07	252.02	7.43
46.		80 Industrial machinery (others)	2302.0	12.08	206.5	3.66	91.79	2.79
47.		81 Machine tools	773.3	5.20	364.0	8.69	222.96	13.33
48.		82 Office computing equipment	53.6	1.30	104.8	19.21	16.56	4.79
49.		83 Other non-electrical machinery	3771.1	3.48	3382.9	10.69	1047.60	7.39
50.	36	84 Electrical Industrial machinery	813.7	1.64	83.4	0.40	248.51	2.34
51.		85 Electrical wires and cables	639.7	1.72	107.2	1.50	108.43	3.18
52		86 Batteries	744.7	10.79	261.5	7.00	100.96	0.61
53.		87 Electrical Appliances	2856.6	10.07	1228.4	13.60	617.29	18.49
54.		88 Communication Equipment	3446.9	15.16	72.7	1.19	616.22	19.72
55.		89 Other electrical machinery	673.0	8.28	383.1	14.54	182.61	14.80
56.		90 Electronic equipment (incl TV)	3554.4	9.13	112.7	2.24	19.42	1.29
57.	37	91 Ships and boat	2.2	Neg	13.5	0.30	87.54	4.84
58.		92 Rail equipments	649.0	1.67	59.2	0.33	66.69	0.84
59.		93 Motor vehicles	2784.1	2.39	954.8	3.72	794.65	6.08
60.		94 Motor cycle & parts	233.9	0.62	44.8	0.48	81.83	1.89
61.		95 Bicycles, cycle-rickshaws	260.6	4.14	340.6	6.68	223.39	8.21
62.		96 Other transport equipment	277.8	3.09	63.1	4.68	13.39	2.98
63.	38	97 Watches and clocks	58.5	0.83	14.9	0.82	16.99	0.99
64.		98 Miscellaneous manufacturing	29841.1	3.62	11155.7	33.03	3484.83	23.97
65.		Total: Sectors 35 to 98	231151.9		70687.3		44246.60	

Source: Same as Table 4.5

Note: Neg stands for Negligible.

Appendix 2 : South Asia: Ratified Coventions

Bangladesh

C 1 Hours of Work (Industry) Convention, 1919 :Ratified on 22:06:72

C 4 Night Work (Women) Convention, 1919 :Ratified on 22:06:72

C 6 Night Work of Young Persons (Industry) Convention, 1919 :Ratified on 22:06:72

C 11 Right of Association (Agriculture) Convention, 1921 Ratified on 22:06:72

C 14 Weekly Rest (Industry) Convention, 1921 Ratified on 22:06:72

C 15 Minimum Age (Trimmers and Stokers) Convention, 1921 Ratified on 22:06:72

C 16 Medical Examination of Young Persons (Sea) Convention, 1921 Ratified on 22:06:72

C 18 Workmen's Compensation (Occupational Diseases) Convention, 1925 Ratified on 2:06:72

C 19 Equality of Treatment (Accident Compensation) Convention, 1925 Ratified on 22:06:72

C 21 Inspection of Emigrants Convention, 1926 Ratified on 22:06:72

C 22 Seamen's Articles of Agreement Convention, 1926 Ratified on 22:06:72

C 27 Marking of Weight (Packages Transported by Vessels) Convention, 1929 Ratified on 22:06:72

C 29 FORCED LABOUR CONVENTION, 1930 Ratified on 22:06:72

C 32 Protection Against Accidents (Dockers) Convention (Revised) Ratified on 2:06:72

C 45 Underground Work (Women) Convention, 1935 Ratified on 22:06:72

C 59 Minimum Age (Industry) Convention (Revised), 1937 Ratified on 22:06:72

C 80 Final Articles Revision Convention, 1946 Ratified on 22:06:72

C 81 Labour Inspection Convention, 1947 Ratified on 22:06:72

C 87 FREEDOM OF ASSOCIATION AND PROTECTION OF THE RIGHT TO ORGANISE CONVENTION, 1948 Ratified on 22:06:72

C 100 Equal Remuneration Convention, 1951 Ratified on 28:01:98

C 89 Night Work (Women) Convention (Revised), 1948 Ratified on 22:06:72

C 90 Night Work Of Young Persons (Industry) Convention (Revised), 1948 Ratified on 22:06:72

C 96 Fee-Charging Employment Agencies Convention (Revised), 1949 Ratified on 22:06:72

C 98 RIGHT TO ORGANISE AND COLLECTIVE BARGAINING CONVENTION, 1949 Ratified on 22:06:72

C 105 ABOLITION OF FORCED LABOUR CONVENTION, 1957 Ratified on 22:06:72

C 106 Weekly Rest (Commerce And Offices) Convention, 1957 Ratified on 22:06:72

C 107 Indigenous And Tribal Populations Convention, 1957 Ratified on 22:06:72

C 111 DISCRIMINATION (EMPLOYMENT AND OCCUPATION) CONVENTION, 1958 Ratified on 22:06:72

C 116 Final Articles Revision Convention, 1961 Ratified on 22:06:72

C 118 Equality Of Treatment (Social Security) Convention, 1962 Ratified on 22:06:72

C 144 TRIPARTITE CONSULTATION (INTERNATIONAL LABOUR STANDARDS) CONVENTION, 1976 Ratified on 17:04:79

C 149 Nursing Personnel Convention, 1977 Ratified on 17:04:79

India

C 1 Hours of Work (Industry) Convention, 1919 Ratified on 14:07:21

C 2 Unemployment Convention, 1919 Ratified on 14:07:21 Ratification denounced

C 4 Night Work (Women) Convention, 1919 Ratified on 14:07:21

C 5 Minimum Age (Industry) Convention, 1919 Ratified on 09:09:55

C 6 Night Work of Young Persons (Industry) Convention, 1919 Ratified on 14:07:21

C 11 Right of Association (Agriculture) Convention, 1921 Ratified on 11:05:23

C 14 Weekly Rest (Industry) Convention, 1921 Ratified on 11:05:23

C 15 Minimum Age (Trimmers and Stokers) Convention, 1921 Ratified on 20:11:22

C 16 Medical Examination of Young Persons (Sea) Convention, 1921 Ratified on 20:11:22

C 18 Workmen's Compensation (Occupational Diseases) Convention, 1925 Ratified on 30:09:27

C 19 Equality of Treatment (Accident Compensation) Convention, 1925 Ratified on 30:09:27

C 21 Inspection of Emigrants Convention, 1926 Ratified on 14:01:28

C 22 Seamen's Articles of Agreement Convention, 1926 Ratified on 31:10:32

C 26 Minimum Wage-Fixing Machinery Convention, 1928 Ratified on 10:01:55

C 27 Marking of Weight (Packages Transported by Vessels) Convention, 1929 Ratified on 07:09:31

C 29 FORCED LABOUR CONVENTION, 1930 Ratified on 30:11:54

C 32 Protection Against Accidents (Dockers) Convention (Revised), 1932 Ratified on 10:02:47

C 41 Night Work (Women) Convention (Revised), 1934 Ratified on 22:11:35 Ratification denounced

C 42 Workmen's Compensation (Occupational Diseases) Convention (Revised), 1934 Ratified on 13:01:64

C 45 Underground Work (Women) Convention, 1935 Ratified on 25:03:38

C 80 Final Articles Revision Convention, 1946 Ratified On 17:11:47

C 81 Labour Inspection Convention, 1947 Ratified on 07:04:49

C 88 Employment Service Convention, 1948 Ratified on 24:06:59

C 89 Night Work (Women) Convention (Revised), 1948 Ratified on 27:02:50

C 90 Night Work Of Young Persons (Industry) Convention (Revised), 1948 Ratified on 27:02:50

C 100 EQUAL REMUNERATION CONVENTION, 1951 Ratified on 25:09:58

C 107 Indigenous And Tribal Populations Convention, 1957 Ratified on 29:09:58

C 111 DISCRIMINATION (EMPLOYMENT AND OCCUPATION) CONVENTION, 1958 Ratified on 03:06:60

C 115 Radiation Protection Convention, 1960 Ratified on 17:11:75

C 116 Final Articles Revision Convention, 1961 Ratified on 21:06:62

C 118 Equality Of Treatment (Social Security) Convention, 1962 Ratified on 19:08:64

C 123 Minimum Age (Underground Work) Convention, 1965 Ratified on 20:03:75

C 136 Benzene Convention, 1971 Ratified on 11:06:91

C 141 Rural Workers' Organizations Convention, 1975 Ratified on 18:08:77

C 144 TRIPARTITE CONSULTATION (INTERNATIONAL LABOUR STANDARDS) CONVENTION, 1976 Ratified on 27:02:78

C 160 Labour Statistics Convention, 1985 Ratified on 01:04:92

C 147 Merchant Shipping (Minimum Standards) Convention, 1976 Ratified on 26:09:96

Pakistan

C 1 Hours of Work (Industry) Convention, 1919 Ratified on 14:07:21

C 4 Night Work (Women) Convention, 1919 Ratified on 14:07:21

C 6 Night Work of Young Persons (Industry) Convention, 1919 Ratified on 14:07:21

C 11 Right of Association (Agriculture) Convention, 1921 Ratified on 11:05:23

C 14 Weekly Rest (Industry) Convention, 1921 Ratified on 11:05:23

C 15 Minimum Age (Trimmers and Stokers) Convention, 1921 Ratified on 20:11:22

C 16 Medical Examination of Young Persons (Sea) Convention, 1921 Ratified on 20:11:22

C 18 Workmen's Compensation (Occupational Diseases) Convention, 1925 Ratified on 30:09:27

C 19 Equality of Treatment (Accident Compensation) Convention, 1925 Ratified on 30:09:27

C 21 Inspection of Emigrants Convention, 1926 Ratified on 14:01:28

C 22 Seamen's Articles of Agreement Convention, 1926 Ratified on 31:10:32

C 27 Marking of Weight (Packages Transported by Vessels) Convention, 1929 Ratified on 07:09:31

C 29 FORCED LABOUR CONVENTION, 1930 Ratified on 23:12:57

C 32 Protection Against Accidents (Dockers) Convention (Revised), 1932 Ratified on 10:02:47

C 41 Night Work (Women) Convention (Revised), 1934 Ratified on 22:11:35 Ratification denounced

C 45 Underground Work (Women) Convention, 1935 Ratified on 25:03:38

C 59 Minimum Age (Industry) Convention (Revised), 1937 Ratified on 26:05:55

C 80 Final Articles Revision Convention, 1946 Ratified on 25:03:48

C 81 Labour Inspection Convention, 1947 Ratified on 10:10:53

C 87 FREEDOM OF ASSOCIATION AND PROTECTION OF THE RIGHT TO ORGANISE CONVENTION, 1948 Ratified on 14:02:51

C 89 Night Work (Women) Convention (Revised), 1948 Ratified on 14:02:51

C 90 Night Work Of Young Persons (Industry) Convention (Revised), 1948 Ratified on 14:02:51

C 96 Fee-Charging Employment Agencies Convention (Revised), 1949 Ratified on 26:05:52

C 98 RIGHT TO ORGANISE AND COLLECTIVE BARGAINING CONVENTION, 1949 Ratified on 26:05:52

C105 ABOLITION OF FORCED LABOUR CONVENTION, 1957 Ratified on 15:02:60

C106 Weekly Rest (Commerce And Offices) Convention, 1957 Ratified on 15:02:60

C107 Indigenous And Tribal Populations Convention, 1957 Ratified on 15:02:60

C111 DISCRIMINATION (EMPLOYMENT AND OCCUPATION) CONVENTION, 1958 Ratified on 24:01:61

C 116 Final Articles Revision Convention, 1961 Ratified on 17:11:67

C 118 Equality Of Treatment (Social Security) Convention, 1962 Ratified on 27:03:69

C 144 TRIPARTITE CONSULTATION (INTERNATIONAL LABOUR STANDARDS) CONVENTION, 1976 Ratified on 25:10:94

C 159 Vocational Rehabilitation and Employment (Disabled Persons) Convention, 1983 Ratified on 25:10:94

Sri Lanka

C 4 Night Work (Women) Convention, 1919 Ratified on 08:10:51 Ratification denounced

C 5 Minimum Age (Industry) Convention, 1919 Ratified on 27:09:51

C 6 Night Work of Young Persons (Industry) Convention, 1919 Ratified on 26:10:50 Ratification denounced

C 7 Minimum Age (Sea) Convention, 1920 Ratified on 02:09:50

C 8 Unemployment Indemnity (Shipwreck) Convention, 1920 Ratified on 25:04:51

C 11 Right of Association (Agriculture) Convention, 1921 Ratified on 25:08:52

C 15 Minimum Age (Trimmers and Stokers) Convention, 1921 Ratified on 25:04:51

C 16 Medical Examination of Young Persons (Sea) Convention, 1921Ratified on 25:04:51

C 18 Workmen's Compensation (Occupational Diseases) Convention, 1925 Ratified on 17:05:52

C 26 Minimum Wage-Fixing Machinery Convention, 1928 Ratified on 09:06:71

C 29 FORCED LABOUR CONVENTION, 1930 Ratified on 05:04:50

C 41 Night Work (Women) Convention (Revised), 1934 Ratified on 02:09:50 Ratification denounced

C 45 Underground Work (Women) Convention, 1935 Ratified on 20:12:50

C 58 Minimum Age (Sea) Convention (Revised), 1936 Ratified on 18:05:59

C 63 Convention Concerning Statistics Of Wages And Hours Of Work, 1938 Ratified on 25:08:52 Ratification denounced on 01:04:93

C 80 Final Articles Revision Convention, 1946 Ratified on 19:09:50

C 81 Labour Inspection Convention, 1947 Ratified on 03:04:56

C 89 Night Work (Women) Convention (Revised), 1948 Ratified on 31:03:66 Ratification denounced

C 90 Night Work Of Young Persons (Industry) Convention (Revised), 1948 Ratified on 18:05:59

C 95 Protection Of Wages Convention, 1949 Ratified on 27:10:83

C 96 Fee-Charging Employment Agencies Convention (Revised), 1949 Ratified on 30:04:58

C 98 RIGHT TO ORGANISE AND COLLECTIVE BARGAINING CONVENTION, 1949 Ratified on 13:12:72

C 99 Minimum Wage Fixing Machinery (Agriculture) Convention, 1951 Ratified on 05:04:54

C 106 Weekly Rest (Commerce And Offices) Convention, 1957 Ratified on 27:10:83

C 115 Radiation Protection Convention, 1960 Ratified on 18:06:86

C 116 Final Articles Revision Convention, 1961 Ratified on 26:04:74

C 131 Minimum Wage Fixing Convention, 1970 Ratified on 17:03:75

C 135 Workers' Representatives Convention, 1971 Ratified on 16:11:76

C 10 Minimum Age (Agriculture) Convention, 1921 Ratified on 29:11:91

C 100 EQUAL REMUNERATION CONVENTION, 1951 Ratified on 01:04:93

C 103, Maternity Protection Convention (Revised), 1952 Ratified on 01:04:93

C 160 Labour Statistics Convention, 1985 Ratified on 01:04:93

C 144 Tripartite Consultation (International Labour Standards) Convention, 1976 Ratified on 17:03:94

C 87 Freedom of Association and Protection of the Right to Organise Convention, 1948 Ratified on 15:09:95

C 108 Seafarers' Identity Documents Convention, 1958Ratified on 24:11:95
C 110 Plantations Convention, 1958 Ratified on 24:04:95

Nepal

C 14 Weekly Rest (Industry) Convention, 1921 Ratified on 10:12:86
C 100 EQUAL REMUNERATION CONVENTION, 1951 Ratified on
    10:06:76
C 111 DISCRIMINATION (EMPLOYMENT AND OCCUPATION)
    CONVENTION, 1958 Ratified on 19:09:74
C 131 Minimum Wage Fixing Convention, 1970 Ratified on 19:09:74
C 144 Tripartite Consultation (International Labour Standards) Convention,
    1976 Ratified on 21:03:95
C 98 Right to Organise and Collective Bargaining Convention, 1949 Ratified
    on 11:11:96
C 138 MINIMUM AGE CONVENTION, 1973 Ratified on 30:05:97

Source: International Labour Organization : ILOLEX